THE
PRESSURE
CANNING
COOKBOOK

THE
PRESSURE
CANNING
COOKBOOK

STEP-BY-STEP RECIPES FOR PANTRY
STAPLES, GUT-HEALING BROTHS,
MEAT, FISH, AND MORE

JENNIFER GOMES,
MASTER FOOD PRESERVER

Skyhorse Publishing

Skyhorse Publishing books may be purchased in bulk at special discounts for
sales promotion, corporate gifts, fund-raising, or educational purposes. Special
editions can also be created to specifications. For details, contact the Special Sales
Department, Skyhorse Publishing, 307 West 36th Street, 11th Floor, New York, NY
10018 or info@skyhorsepublishing.com.

Skyhorse® and Skyhorse Publishing® are registered trademarks of Skyhorse
Publishing, Inc.®, a Delaware corporation.

Visit our website at www.skyhorsepublishing.com.

10 9 8 7 6 5 4 3 2 1

Library of Congress Cataloging-in-Publication Data is available on file.

Cover design by Kai Texel
Cover photos by Della Hayden

Print ISBN: 978-1-5107-7625-8
Ebook ISBN: 978-1-5107-7626-5

Printed in China

*To my children and husband for taste testing and tolerating
a steamy kitchen in the heat of summer. I love you.*

CONTENTS

INTRODUCTION

MY PRESSURE CANNING JOURNEY

I grew up in a lush, rural, agricultural valley in the mountains of Northern California, where I now make my home. My mom and grandmother water-bath canned the vegetables from our garden and fruit from the many fruit trees on our family ranch, all of which had been planted and tended to decades before by my industrious great grandmother. I helped by picking fruit—often climbing limbs of apple trees or reaching from the back of a pickup into the upper vines of wild blackberry bushes—and prepping the produce. Many kids I knew back then came to school with scratched arms and purple fingertips in August and September (just like me), but each year I really looked forward to picking berries with child-hood friends who lived nearby.

My first food preservation love was water-bath canning. Having been raised on a cattle ranch, I now see that my mom and grandmother canned out of necessity, in order to preserve the harvest of their vegetable gardens and the bounty of fruit weighing down the branches of the ranch's fruit trees.

Because of our cattle-rearing—and subsequent cattle-eating back-ground—we were chest freezer people. Every family I knew who raised cattle also had a chest freezer, and sometimes more than one. A large, dedicated freezer was a necessary expense for keeping a whole or half steer for the many months after butchering. I believe this is why my family didn't pressure can. We already had a means: a freezer plugged in and waiting to preserve meat.

When I met my husband, a young man from a logging background, he eagerly encouraged me to learn to pressure can. As an avid hunter, he knew the venison (buck meat, as we refer to it locally) of each season's harvest could be canned—deliciously, I eventually learned—to be enjoyed long after the hunt was over. I heard about how his relatives canned this meat in a variety of ways: with tomato paste, or sliced and seasoned ready for fajitas, or first browned and then canned, ready for a hot sandwich.

A few more buck seasons passed before I first tried my hand at pressure canning, and I was astounded at how easy it was. I simply had to follow the directions included in the box of my new pressure canner and, magically, I did it! There seemed to be so little guesswork, and 100 percent success, I wondered why people had cautioned me before beginning.

Years later, pregnant and my nesting instinct in high gear, I realized (in a panic that only a pregnant woman can imagine) I had nothing on the shelves fit to feed my unborn baby. Never mind that I had at least a full twelve months before this baby could eat any solid food; I was struck by the thought that I needed to start canning, immediately, so my baby would have wholesome jars of unadulterated baby food.

I started with applesauce, which thankfully was an easy beginner preserve. And though there was a lot of trial and even more error, I canned one hundred pounds of apples into applesauce . . . and I was on my canning way!

With that pregnancy, I also became a label reader. I realized that so much of what we eat has added ingredients that are at best unnecessary and at worst not good for our bodies. In shopping for canning books, I found a few good ones, but also several duds. At the time, there was very little online information that seemed up to date, and even more disappointing (at least to me, since I was a working soon-to-be mom), most of it was directed at stay-at-home women who didn't work.

By that I mean, everything I read about preserving seemed to be giant batch recipes, and called for tools that took up a ton of space and were difficult to source. Also, very few recipes felt fresh, new, exciting, or creative.

The more I canned, the more I wanted to bring the message of modern canning to women like me. I am an English teacher, then in a local high school classroom and now at a community college. I wanted recipes that had some flair and would be tasty, healthy, and impress my husband, but that I could preserve while a baby napped.

In my online search, I learned that cooperative extension offices across the country host Master Food Preserver courses where attendees can learn about all kinds of preservation, *including pressure canning*. The closest course to me was a few hours away and several weekends in a row, which was hardly a sensible schedule for a new mom. And according to a local source in her eighties, the last Master Food Preserver in *my* area "died a long time ago."

Not wanting to struggle against the current, I just kept canning, had a second baby, and started my blog, *The Domestic Wildflower*. I began blogging because I wanted to share all my homemade recipes and crafts with anyone who wanted to learn.

Soon, I got my first pressure canner and, following the directions as closely as if I were disassembling a bomb, canned my first jars of venison to great success. *Yay!* I used the pressure canner only during hunting season the first few years I had it, keeping that instruction manual close and never daring to pressure can without it being open and handy on the counter beside the stove.

Every spring, I kept searching for a Master Food Preserver course to attend, but never found one that was remotely close enough, especially with little kids at home to care for. Our children grew, as did my canning repertoire, and in 2021 I made friends online with another canning enthusiast, Anna Cash, the creator of a popular canning-centered blog, *Smart Home Canning*.

Interestingly enough, Anna was not just a Master Food Preserver, she also lived at the mecca of food preservation education: Utah State University Extension. (Utah has robust, active cooperative extension offices all over the state staffed with experts, better than any others I've encountered, for sure.) Both kind *and* deeply versed in all things canning, Anna warmly invited me to attend her local Master Food Preserver course. And not only did I attend the weeklong workshop, but I also made new friends and geeked out about all I was learning about food preservation, particularly about pressure canning. Consequently, I brought the knowledge and experience I gained at her course to my blog and social media followers and began writing this book!

Fun sidenote: Anna and I now cohost a food preservation podcast together called *Perfectly Preserved*.

Now, I pressure can as easily as I water-bath. Pressure canning is part of my regular routine, and I want the same for you readers. This book is designed to help you become confident, capable, efficient, and safe in performing this unique food preserving method.

Sooo, let's pressure can some super tasty *and* healthy meals into jars, shall we?

A FEW FACTS ABOUT CANNING IN GENERAL AND PRESSURE CANNING IN PARTICULAR

It's possible you've heard that canning (whether it be water-bath canning or pressure canning) has a reputation for being dangerous. Maybe you've read a story about some person blowing the lid off a pressure canner (or pressure cooker, which *is* different, and yes, they're frequently mistaken for one another) and pulling broken glass out of the ceiling. These stories, thankfully, are entirely avoidable. By simply and conscientiously following the directions, all such trouble can be left behind as urban legend.

You can trust with certainty the directions included by the manufacturer in a pressure canner's box. They're clear, there are usually helpful illustrations or photos, and my experience has shown me that for the best and safest results, it's imperative to simply follow them.

You see, I cannot tell you in this book how *your* particular canner works (for example, exactly how to tighten the lid, or what the dial will say), but I *can* tell you how they generally work, and I *can*—and will—remind you over and over to *please*, just follow the manufacturer's directions.

On a related note, the pressure canning process itself is trustworthy, because this type of food science has been rigorously time-tested over decades, is readily analyzed with a microscope, not politicized, and is actually easy to understand.

It is a simple fact that the heat inside a properly filled and prepared pressure canner gets hot enough (over 240°F) to kill any spoiler that may be present inside the food in your jars (namely, the botulism spore that produces its toxin in a low-acid and anaerobic environment). Cooking any food over 240°F for a specific amount of time kills the botulism spore.* Done! You don't have to think about it after that point.

Important note: A "rebel canner" gets into dangerous territory indeed when they ignore a recipe's recommendations (which are not a mandate or law, by the way) and attempt to preserve foods that cannot be reliably penetrated by the heat in a home pressure canner. I'll go into more depth about this later, but for now, know that the pressure canning process is safe and simple if you commit to following the instructions with care and consistency.

Many years after pressure canning my cute boyfriend's buck meat, I have a family with him. We have two discerning children who test (and sometimes veto) everything I make. This book became my meal planning guide, as I tested, adjusted, and retested each recipe to ensure my kids' and husband's unanimous approval. I believe any of these recipes will be something you'll proudly serve to your family or give as a gift.

Freezers are great. Water-bath canning is wonderful. But pressure canning is uniquely suited for preserving whole and nearly whole meals—soups, stews, broths, and more—into jars, which are then ready whenever you need them . . . *and* they'll be preserved indefinitely without the requirement of refrigeration!

---

* All legitimate pressure canning recipes will state how many minutes are required—it's up to *you* to precisely follow the amount of time specified in each recipe's instructions.

Another benefit to pressure canning? It can alleviate the stress of rising food costs, empty store shelves, and help us refocus on one of our most immediate early evening concerns: *What's for supper?* On a related note, pressure canning can allow you to preserve food when it's at its cheapest and freshest.

The fact is, I'm so glad you're here and I'm hoping that, with practice and the guidance and encouragement I offer in this book, you'll be delighted you learned this unendingly useful technique of pressure canning.

In the following pages, you'll find clear and simple explanations of what pressure canning is—and what it's not—plus, how to use a pressure canner, how to know if recipes you find outside this book are safe, and a wide variety of practical, dependable, and delicious recipes you can preserve immediately. You'll also get my very best tips for making this incredible food preservation technique fit into your daily life!

PART I

Chapter 1

THE BASICS OF PRESSURE CANNING (AND WHY YOU'LL LOVE IT!)

THE NUTS AND BOLTS OF PRESSURE CANNING, INCLUDING SOME ESSENTIAL REQUIREMENTS FOR SAFETY'S SAKE

Pressure canning takes place inside a pressure canner, which is a pot with a locking lid and a dial that tells you how much pressure is inside the pot. Locking this lid allows pressure to build inside the pot, driving the temperature up and over the temperature of boiling water (which is universally and always 212°F, no matter if it's a simmer or a rolling boil, whether it's for five minutes or five days) to between 240° and 250°F.

This high temperature of penetrating, wet heat provides the "magic" of the pressure canner. Why? Because it's in that range (240° to 250°F) that the *Clostridium botulinum* spore (a.k.a. "C. botulinum") and any other food-borne pathogen is killed and thus will never be able to produce its toxin— the toxin which causes the potentially fatal disease known as botulism.

The pressure is what creates the heat, and with that heat it is possible to safely preserve a huge variety of low-acid foods, those which are *not* safe to preserve in a regular water-bath canner (due to insufficient heat).

Whether canning in a water-bath or pressure canner, another important element, besides heat, is acid. Any foods we're wanting to preserve have a pH or acid value. Low numbers denote a highly acidic food. For example, lemons are about a 2 on the pH scale, raspberries a 3, and tomatoes near a 4.5. The critical pH value for every type of canning is 4.6. Any recipe with a pH value of more than 4.6 *must* be pressure canned. (For your protection and safety while canning, I suggest you repeat this last sentence out loud and remember it!)

High-acid recipes (4.6 or lower) innately have an environment where "spoilers" (microorganisms) cannot live, simply because they're too acidic. High acidity coupled with the heat of a boiling water bath (212°F) is enough to drive oxygen out of the jar and kill any spoilers present.

However, those recipes that are more alkaline and less acidic (4.6 or higher) *must* be pressure canned. The botulism toxin in particular can *only* grow in an anaerobic (no-oxygen) *and* low-acid environment. A sealed jar creates that no-oxygen environment it needs to grow, so a low-acid food *must* be heated over 240°F in order to ensure any botulism spores are killed.

You see, C. botulinum spores are present in our soils, on the surface of most fresh foods, and, in fact, all around us. But because they grow only in the absence of air, they are harmless on fresh foods, and are only dangerous—in the context of food preservation—in a no-oxygen and low-acid environment.

Significant testing has been done by the United States Department of Agriculture (USDA), Cooperative Extension Service, and National Center for Home Food Preservation, and it has been determined that pressure canning is a surefire way to heat the food in your jars over that critical temperature of 240°F.

Testing has also shown that water-bath canning low-acid recipes is an unreliable method for heating your foods in jars over 240°F. It's worth noting that the practice of water-bath canning low-acid recipes for a very long time (three hours is common) can be particularly problematic because it's creating the very environment the botulism toxin needs to grow: a sealed jar with no oxygen and not a guarantee of enough heat to kill the C. botulinum spore.

It's also worth noting that there are relatively few cases of botulism poisoning in America each year (about two thousand annually, and most of those are due to raw honey consumption in infants rather than from home canned foods). Still, it's my position that canning unsafely (that is, failing to properly preserve by using a pressure canner when appropriate) is dangerous and discourages new canners from learning safe canning practices.

Clearly, the risk of canning unsafely is unnecessary, and getting sick from botulism is a fate I wouldn't wish on anyone! Once you become familiar with pressure canning, you'll see how silly it is to skip it in favor of water-bath canning.

Indeed, low-acid "recipes" indicating that you skip pressure canning in favor of water-bath canning typically call for a three-hour processing time. Nearly all pressure canning recipes process in ninety minutes, and many recipes can be processed in under an hour. In my mind, it makes no sense to can unsafely *and* more slowly by using a water-bath canner for low-acid foods.

Furthermore, the textual evidence citing a three-hour processing time for water-bath canning low-acid recipes is decades old. By using up-to-date information, as well as modern, safe pressure canning techniques, you'll not only can safely, but you'll also do it faster.

THE IMPORTANCE OF PRESSURE AND TIME IN PRESSURE CANNING (AND MY POV ABOUT GAUGES)

The amount of pressure inside a pressure canner and the corresponding heat is measured by a weighted gauge or a dial gauge, depending on the make and model of pressure canner. Perhaps it's my screen-loving generation and what I'm used to (I normally use a dial gauge) or maybe just my information-seeking personality, but I find the weighted gauge to *feel* like I'm not getting enough information or control from it.

Please don't misunderstand me; pressure canners equipped with a weighted gauge are effective and safe, when calibrated correctly. (Note: I strongly suggest having your local university cooperative extension office— i.e., the government office in your region devoted to rural area revitalization, support of families and communities, food safety and preservation, gardening, and research—check your dial yearly.)

But when a recipe calls for me to preserve at twelve pounds of pressure because of my elevation, I want to preserve *precisely* at twelve pounds of pressure. The fact is, though, due to how it's constructed, a weighted gauge pressure canner *requires* you to preserve at either five, ten, or fifteen pounds of pressure, as there is no option for pounds of canning pressure in between those numbers.

For this reason (and another I'll mention), I tend to like the dial-gauge pressure canner, where I can see a dial (dare I say, like on a screen!) and exactly what the pounds of pressure are inside the pressure canner. This unique feature also prevents the possibility of foods being very slightly overprocessed, i.e., at a higher number of pounds of pressure than what's necessary.

From a safety perspective, however, there's no problem at all with having foods processed at a greater number of "pounds of pressure" than what's necessary. Remember, with a weighted-gauge pressure canner, it's solely up to you to adjust the heat (until steam is released from the vent) in order to adjust the amount of pressure inside.

Interestingly, the brand named "All American" makes pressure canners that have a dial gauge *and* a weighted gauge. Their dial is for reference only, though, as the weighted gauge does the "work" of maintaining pressure (via the release of steam previously mentioned). If you purchase and use an All American pressure canner, I suggest comparing the dial with the weighted gauge. If the dial indicates ten pounds of pressure, but the weighted gauge is set on fifteen pounds, your dial needs to be calibrated so it's reading accurately. If the dial is more than two pounds off, it needs to be calibrated, which you can have done at your nearest cooperative extension office, by the manufacturer, or by a tire shop in a pinch. This will then provide you with both indicators of pressure.

So, which type of pressure canner do I recommend? While I personally prefer my dial-gauge canner (again, it's what I'm used to!), a weighted-gauge canner is wonderful, as well. The All American, which is considered the "gold standard" in pressure canners, gives you both the dial and the weighted gauge and further solidifies its place at the head of the pack.

Now that you understand the difference between the two types of pressure canners, find one that fits your needs and budget, works well, and has a manual. What's most important to me, though, is to find a well-functioning (that is, brand new or used *but in great condition*) pressure canner that has a readily available instruction manual *and* fits your size needs (pot sizes vary, so the amount of food you intend to preserve through pressure canning ought to be considered before making your purchase). If you follow this approach, I sincerely believe you'll learn to love whichever type you end up choosing, whether it's a weight-gauge pressure canner or a dial-gauge pressure canner.

A FEW MORE NOTES WHEN COMPARING PRESSURE CANNING AND WATER-BATH CANNING

All pressure canning recipes indicate an amount of time that recipes are to be processed at a particular number of pounds of pressure. By comparison, each water-bath canning recipe calls for a specific amount of time to be processed. That's because the heat is always 212°F in a boiling water bath.

In a pressure canner, the heat is over 240°F and up to 250°F. At sea level, pressure canning recipes are processed at eleven pounds of pressure. As elevation increases, so do the pounds per pressure required. However, the processing time remains the same whether at sea level or on top of Mount Everest!

This is a key difference that water-bath canners will notice; the time of processing doesn't change with elevation when pressure canning—but the number of pounds of pressure does. Another difference between the two canning methods is that pressure canning takes a bit longer because of the types of foods appropriate for this method. These include low-acid foods like meats, vegetables, and beans, which are all fairly dense, thereby needing greater heat for a longer period of time in order to raise their internal temperature to over 240°F—the temperature required to kill any C botulinum bacteria that could be present. It should be noted that pressure canning recipes are rarely processed for longer than ninety minutes.

The types of foods you can pressure can are vast, and when you read this book's extensive list of recipes that can be safely preserved in a pressure canner, you'll see that there are countless variations to explore, and that the longer processing times required (compared to high-acid water-bath canning recipes) make it a worthy investment.

JARS AND SUCH

Another consideration is the size of the jar. It is common to water-bath can in half-pint jars (think of a typical jam jar), which are appropriate—from tiny 4-ounce jars of hot sauce up to half gallons of cranberry juice. Typically, it isn't practical to pressure can smaller jars, simply because of the types of recipes—half a cup of broth or stew isn't particularly useful, but two or four cups are much more so. Therefore, the standard jars used for pressure canning are pints or quarts.

However, when pressure canning fish, it's common to preserve in half pints or pints. So, in this book, I provide no times or instructions for preserving fish in *quarts*. This is because the processing times for fish are so great (one hundred minutes) and testing has indicated that it's safest to can (and thus penetrate with heat the interior of a smaller jar) in half pints or pints for fish. To be clear, processing times—all around the world—are determined by the time it takes for the heat of the pressure canner to penetrate the particular recipe, considering the density of the foods therein, and are specific to the jar size.

A LITTLE BIT ABOUT JAR HEADSPACE

Just as the times to process vary from water-bath canning to pressure canning, so do the amounts of headspace required. Headspace is the distance from the top of the jar to the top of the food being preserved. In water-bath canning, the distance can be as little as a quarter of an inch, and as much as one inch, and vary between recipes.

But, in pressure canning, it is most common to have a headspace of one inch and sometimes an inch and a half. Headspace is important because the processing time (and pressure) in pressure canning works to drive oxygen out of the jar, which will create that essential vacuum seal. Therefore, the amount of headspace is part of that crucial equation.

SOME DOS & DON'TS WHEN FILLING JARS

Invariably you'll run into a quandary when you don't have enough preserve to fill a jar to the one-inch (or as specified) headspace. Please note: You should *not* preserve a jar with less, *or* more, than the specified headspace. This headspace is needed to create the vacuum seal. If you have less, simply put a used lid on the jar, set it in a reusable container, and refrigerate. It's always better to be safe than sorry!

THE BOTTOM LINE ABOUT PRESSURE CANNING

As I relayed earlier, pressure canning opens up a wide world of possibilities for safe food preservation and really rounds out a preserver's skill set! Having an understanding of water-bath canning can be helpful when learning how to pressure can, but it certainly isn't a requirement. I will say, though, that knowing the difference between the two methods can be impactful, as you may encounter well-intended but inaccurate advice referencing one method, yet failing to take into consideration vital nuances between the two.

I want to reiterate this to you: *Pressure canning is easy to do!* Yes, it requires a pressure canner (of course), but not a lot of other equipment. And sure, canned jams, fruits, and pickles are great, but pressure canning allows you to preserve hearty meals into jars, which are shelf-stable and delicious for a year or more! The investment time it takes to pressure can be greater, but so is the reward.

WHEN PRESSURE CANNING IS NOT APPROPRIATE

While I hope you read this book as a celebration of the joy of pressure canning a great many tasty and nutritious low-acid recipes, it isn't appropriate for every food—fortunately, it's relatively few, compared to the huge number of foods that *can* be safely preserved through pressure canning.

Believe me, though, you're best off heeding the established standards and avoiding pressure canning the few foods that should *not* be pressure canned, even if your neighbor, grandmother, or some person on social media did. Ignore the noise online and simply follow tested methods, like those described in this book.

By the way, since there's a lot of info out there about canning pumpkin, here are the specifics about this somewhat tricky fruit. (Yep, it's botanically categorized as a fruit, not a vegetable!)

Pumpkin puree is a food that should never be pressure canned, due to its density. Pumpkin cubes, however, *can* be pressure canned (cubes allow for heat to flow all the way around them), *but* the result is a mush of a cube. And I personally don't see a reason to can mushy cubes of pumpkin.

A NOTE ABOUT CANNING PUMPKIN

When it comes to pressure canning, pumpkin and winter squash have some very specific rules. Pumpkin *puree* should never be canned at home. It's too dense for heat to reliably penetrate. If you wonder how cans of pureed pumpkin came to be (i.e., the kind you find ready and waiting on grocery store shelves for Thanksgiving), it's due to commercial canners being as big as whole rooms and getting much, much hotter than your at-home pressure canner. Pumpkin and winter squash can be safely pressure canned only by using the following method. Pumpkins or winter squash should be washed and peeled. Then, the flesh should be cut into 1-inch cubes. The cubes must then be boiled for 2 minutes and drained, taking great care to not mash the cubes. Fill your hot jars with these parboiled cubes and the water in which you cooked them, leaving 1 inch of headspace. The processing times are 55 minutes for pints and 90 minutes for quarts, at 11 pounds of pressure. Personally, I have no use for soft cubes of canned pumpkin and find that a better method of preservation is freezing. Choose your method but stay away from any pureed pumpkin or squash "recipes."

Freezing or freeze drying are better options for pumpkin puree, as well as pumpkin cubes, and the same goes for a few other vegetables (see on next page).

Why? These foods *all* have issues with heat failing to penetrate due to density and/or providing a subpar result after pressure canning. Consider instead the effectiveness of dehydrating these foods. The positive results of dehydrating these veggies are they're lighter in terms of weight, have a smaller shelf footprint, and are easily rehydrated in soups, etc. Consider freezing or drying the following foods, as they have both a better, more delicious result by using those methods, and when pressure canned, they have issues with proper heat penetration:

- Broccoli
- Brussel sprouts
- Cabbage
- Cauliflower
- Kohlrabi
- Turnips
- Rutabagas
- Mashed potatoes
- Summer squash, including zucchini, yellow squash, and spaghetti squash

Finally, there are a few food groups that are entirely off-limits for safe home canning. Grains (breads, muffins, flour for dredging or thickening, etc.) are not safe for *any* type of canning. Milk products (both dairy and nondairy milk, cheese, butter, cream, and more) are *also* not safe for pressure canning. Note: You can always add cream, butter, sour cream, cheese, or milk *at the re-heating step*, if those ingredients are desired. Mexican Bean and Bone Soup (see recipe on page 116), for example, is delicious when reheated with shredded cheese and a dollop of sour cream. But I repeat: *Never can dairy or grains*.

At the time of this book's publication, the majority of new nondairy milks (almond, oat, cashew, etc.) have not been tested for use in pressure canning, so it would be best *not* to use—or substitute in any way—those ingredients in pressure canning recipes. Add those ingredients to your heart's content when you reheat pressure canning recipes instead . . . and you'll *never* have to question the safety of your canning practice.

A very good question I often hear is, "Why can't I just pressure can everything?" You *could* use a pressure canner to preserve water-bath canning recipes but doing so would likely yield safely preserved mush. You now may be wondering, *Why is that?* Many high-acid recipes, when processed at over 240°F temperature in a pressure canner, will give you a result that you'd really never enjoy eating. (As I said, "mush.") So yes, you could, theoretically, preserve all canning recipes in a pressure canner . . . but it's completely unnecessary for high-acid foods to be preserved in this manner and, in many cases, it would take longer, too.

The most important ingredient in any pressure canning expedition—and by now this may not surprise you at all—is *you*. Pressure canning requires . . . nay, it demands that you follow directions closely. Fortunately, the directions for pressure canning are not difficult. They are not mysterious. And I'll do my very best to explain the why and the how of every aspect of pressure canning—including all the wonderful recipes I've created here for you—in clear, simple language throughout the rest of this book.

At this point, I want to emphasize, above all, you must follow each of the directions in order to safely pressure can. If you remember just one thing from this book, may it be that you follow the directions, particularly those provided by the manufacturer of your pressure canner.

In literally every pressure canner's original box you should find a specific set of directions for that model: clear, step-by-step directions for how to properly fill, exhaust, and preserve using that particular canner. (Many, if not all, new pressure canners will also include a handful of basic recipes in the box.)

By learning to properly pressure can, you'll gain expertise in preserving whole, delicious, homemade meals in jars, which can be enjoyed a jar at a time, free from preservatives, pesticides, or chemicals. If you're feeling ready and eager, it's time to read on!

JARS YOU CAN USE FOR PRESSURE CANNING

The ubiquitous mason-style canning jar seems as American as apple pie and baseball. This is a great choice for pressure canning. *Always* use mason-style jars with *new* canning lids. The rings (also known as bands) can be reused over and over, as with the jars. However, it's best to get into the habit of checking all of your jars for chips or cracks before beginning any batch to avoid a broken jar. Trust me, your food preserving heart will be broken to match if a jar cracks mid-processing. Besides that, it's a mess, as well as a darn shame to lose a jar of food that way!

Processing time will dictate the appropriate size of the jar you use, and it's important to use the suggested size or a smaller jar, as the pounds of pressure required is based on the size of the filled jar. If the recipe gives processing directions for quarts, and you want to preserve in pints, that's fine; use the pounds per pressure for quarts, if no other information is given.

WECK jars are German jars that are popular in Europe but seem to be gaining interest in America. They have an all-glass construction, including a glass lid, metal clips that hold the glass lid, and a separate, reusable rubber flange in place during the canning process. They are a bit more expensive than standard mason-style jars, come in many shapes and sizes, have six opening sizes, and are especially beautiful. Additionally, one practical reason you may want to consider them is that they're completely free of plastic; only glass will touch the food inside. These jars are safe for pressure canning but require the use of three clips around the lid (rather than the two required for water-bath canning), arranged evenly around the jar.

To use a WECK jar, place the rubber flange on the upside-down lid (the underside will be facing up on your kitchen table or countertop while you place the rubber flange on it), then place the lid and rubber flange together on top of the jar. Apply clips at that time and use a silicone, grippy oven mitt or a jar lifter designed for the size of jar you're using (practice on a cold jar beforehand!). Be advised, many WECK jars won't quite fit in a standard jar lifter's opening, so check this before beginning the canning process.

Canning jars are a great item to find used at thrift stores, garage sales, flea markets, etc. But again, *always* use new canning lids. (And don't reuse them for any canning purposes.) Also, it should be noted that store-bought jars—for example, mayonnaise, pasta sauce, pickle, and other similar styles—are *not* appropriate jars for canning, as they are not designed to withstand the heat of the canning process and include lids that won't withstand the heat or the pressure involved, nor do they create the tight seal necessary for long-term storage. Helpful hint: Save those mayo, pasta, and pickle jars for *other* household uses; just don't use them for canning.

The largest size jar in any brand of canning-safe jar tested specifically for safe pressure canning is the quart jar. Half-gallon jars should not be used for pressure canning, though are appropriate for water-bath canning high-acid juices, such as grape, apple, and cranberry. And another reminder: You can preserve in jars smaller than the ones listed in the recipe, but not larger, and certainly not larger than a quart in a pressure canner.

A NOTE ABOUT LIDS AND STERILIZATION

When you buy a flat of standard canning jars with lids and rings from a store, it's very possible that all the lids will feel sealed or otherwise be stuck on top of their jars. The heat of transit and pressure of being stacked indefinitely in the backroom of a store can cause jar lids to feel sealed. After asking the Ball company about this, they explained to me that these seemingly "stuck" new lids are still functionally sound, unsealed, and can be used in the canning process. This was a relief to me as nearly every jar in my rural area has traveled a great and surely hot journey before landing in my shopping cart; and these lids always seem to be falsely sealed when I encounter them. Here's my recommendation: Gently lift the lid with your fingers, if possible, or if you must, use a jar opener or similar tool to carefully loosen the edge. With experience, you'll notice that these seals are not the super-strong seal of a proper canning process.

Contrary to what you may have heard or read, lids do not need to be simmered, softened, or heated prior to the pressure canning process. The requirement for simmering and softening lids was removed in the 1970s, as the plastisol flange formula was changed, so even if your mama or grandma used to soften their canning lids, know that you don't need to.

One last note about sterilization: Your jars, lids, and equipment should all be clean, but do not need to be sterilized before canning. The canning process (submersion in pure steam in the pressure canning process and boiling water in the water-bath canning process) sterilizes the inside and outside of your jars in ten minutes. As pressure canning recipes all have a ten minute or longer processing time, you do not need to preboil or presterilize.

FYI: PRESSURE CANNERS ARE *NOT* STEAM CANNERS

Note: The following is to help clarify what pressure canning is and what it's not.

There's a device available for those interested in water-bath canning more quickly, and this typically aluminum analog device is called an atmospheric steam canner. These are not pressure canners. Do not confuse one for the other, as they are not interchangeable. Steam canners bathe jars in steam but are not appropriate for low-acid recipes. Pressure canners bathe jars in steam and raise the temperature to over 240°F, making them appropriate for low-acid recipes. The fastest and easiest way to tell the difference between these types of canners is that a pressure canner is quite heavy, while a steam canner is, generally speaking, lightweight. Furthermore, the lid of a steam canner is like that of a cake dome—it's large and the base is short, while a pressure canner is the reverse, with a deep base and short lid.

Chapter 2

WHAT BRAND OF PRESSURE CANNER SHOULD I BUY?

As with cars, sewing machines, and face cream (among many other things), people have their favorite brands of pressure canners. You may be shopping for a new canner and considering your options, or you may be a thrifting queen searching for a pressure canner for sale at a thrift store for a great price. Here's what I think of as the "big two" brands in the pressure canning world . . . and I will share a bit about each brand, for your consideration.

The All American pressure canners, which of course are made in the USA, are regularly rated to be the "best overall" in annual reviews of pressure canners. They're high quality, very heavy-duty, made of cast aluminum, and are more expensive. While All American is a well-respected brand in the canning community, I think their pressure canners look a bit more intimidating than other styles, particularly because of the screw-style lids, but that should not deter you if you're drawn to buying what many regard as America's top brand. I haven't met anyone who didn't love their All American.

The only drawbacks I could list here are their price, and they have a lot of sizes to choose from, which for a beginner could be overwhelming. All American currently has six models available, and one model is available in six different (very fun!) colors. They feature an exclusive metal-to-metal seal, as opposed to the gasket seal of the Presto brand described below. The 25-quart option is listed for sale at around $450 at the time of this book's publishing. They range in size from 10 to 41 liquid quart capacity.

Presto pressure canners come from an American-based company, as well, but are made in China. Like All American, Presto is also a well-respected name in the canning universe. Presto canners are lighter, and they use a gasket in the lid to create the airtight seal, as opposed to the metal-to-metal connection of the All American. Currently, Presto offers three models, but one of their offerings has a stainless-steel bottom, making it a great (and I believe the only) choice for those with induction cooktops. The largest size Presto makes, 23 quarts, costs $160 at the time of this book's publication.

While Presto only offers the sizes of 16- and 23-quart pressure canners, they also offer a digital pressure canner appliance. These are easily identified because they're black (rather than silver) and have an electrical cord. As they have not made public the research they did to ensure the temperatures inside the jars get hot enough to satisfy the requirements for killing all food-borne pathogens, it is best to use the recipes in the Presto manual *only*, as those are the recipes tested by Presto themselves.

The Presto 16-quart model holds 16 quarts of liquid and 7 quart jars. The only other size available, the 23-quart model, also holds only 7 quarts, but is tall enough to stack pint jars and can accommodate 20 pint jars.

The pressure canner I use and love? Presto's 16-quart model. I'm sure I'd love an All American, but I chose the Presto 16-quart pressure canner because I have a small kitchen, small budget, and small family. If I needed to preserve more low-acid recipes in greater volume, I'd invest in an All American in a larger size or get the 23-quart Presto model.

You should consider your budget, your cabinet space, the size of batches you hope to preserve with your new pressure canner, your stovetop style (conventional or induction), and the availability of the pressure canner you're wanting.

If you can use a pressure canner with a friend before purchasing, do so, and see how you like it before making a decision. Also consider the time it will take to prepare the canner for canning, the process known as "exhausting" the canner. A larger canner will take a bit longer to be ready to exhaust than one with a smaller capacity.

Other brands are less common, so if you consider one, look over the manual closely. Review it for clear recipe and usage directions, a labeled guide for parts and pieces of the canner, and for safety information. There should be a clear way for you to contact them, as well, including an email or website and perhaps a telephone number. Why? Because in the event you need a replacement part, it breaks down, or you want to ask a usage question, for example, you'll need their contact info to reach them.

It should be noted that many pressure canners are marketed as pressure *cookers*, as well, and have the capacity to, and instructions for, pressure cooking. A pressure canner can *also* serve as a water-bath canner. (A water-bath canner can be any pot that has a rack in the bottom that is 2 to 3 inches taller than the tallest jar you'd use.)

For the purposes of this book, I've focused exclusively on an appliance's pressure canning capabilities; but if pressure cooking is another type of cooking you'd like to explore, know that a pressure canner can also serve you in this way. Just be sure to clean all parts (especially the vent port) very well after cooking with your appliance, to ensure a safe pressure canning process the next time you choose to can with it.

For reference, Instant Pot–style appliances are modern iterations of pressure cookers. It used to be very popular to use an analog, locking-lid pressure cooker to cook tougher, cheaper cuts of meat. The pressure canners of today have the critically important dial that indicates the number of pounds of pressure inside needed for pressure canning.

Furthermore, pressure cookers are not always pressure canners. Therefore, be certain you're shopping for a pressure canner to ensure it can be used for that process; but know it may also be used as a pressure cooker. Do *not* buy a pressure cooker and assume it can function as a pressure canner. (It needs to be made clear by the manufacturer that the appliance may be used as a pressure canner.)

DIGITAL CANNING APPLIANCES

There are many digital electric appliances out there marketed for canning. Presto has a digital pressure canner available. And while Presto has not made their research public, they seem to have determined that the appropriate heat has been reached inside their jars during the pressure canning process. Until more testing is done, it is best to use only those recipes.

A number of Instant Pot–style appliances are marketed for pressure canning, as well. At the time of this book's publishing, in testing done by cooperative extension offices, insufficient heat was measured in these devices, particularly when canning above sea level. They are, therefore, not recommended for pressure canning.

The problem I see with digital canning appliances is the inarguable limitations in batch size. You can't fit very many jars in most Instant Pot–style appliances. The fact is, they are not pressure canners; they are pressure cookers with a pressure canning function. However, they don't maintain the heat above 1,000 feet elevation and they're generally too small (in my mind) to use for pressure canning. I think a better investment is a pressure canner that is not digital and that is well-tested and widely used.

Instant Pot–style appliances *can* be valuable tools in preparing your preserves before the pressure canning process takes place. Feel free to cook your meat, beans, or other ingredients in a pressure cooker before the pressure canning process (see more about "hot packing" on page 26) to save time and help make preserving a large batch in a pressure canner more manageable.

STORING YOUR PRESSURE CANNER

A pressure canner should be stored indoors, away from swings in temperature and humidity, preferably in the original box, which would help prevent the dial from being damaged. You may want to store it in the garage or attic when unused, but that's not an ideal location. I keep mine in the original box in a closet next to my shoes. You can put crumpled tissue paper or newspapers in the bottom during storage, as well, to absorb any remaining moisture that may be present after washing.

CALIBRATING THE PRESSURE CANNER DIAL

It is recommended you get your pressure canner's dial checked yearly to confirm it is accurate. Your local cooperative extension office is a free resource available that can test it for you or direct you to a nearby office that can. Cooperative extension offices are mentioned throughout this book for good reason. They are staffed by experts who are passionate about safe food preservation, and they hold a wealth of knowledge. However, many areas don't have a robust cooperative extension near them (my area is one of them), so having your dial tested at such an office isn't feasible. In this case, a good alternative is to have it tested at your local tire shop. They have the tools to measure if the dial is accurately indicating pressure.

This may come as a surprise, but it is best to have even a brand-new pressure canner dial tested before use; just as it's wise to have your trusty pressure canner you've been using for years tested yearly. In my Master Food Preserver course, two attendees each reported having brand-new dials indicate inaccurate pressure when tested. They felt lucky to have had their dials tested, so they could be adjusted before they used them *and* could begin preserving safely.

Chapter 3

THE ESSENTIAL PARTS
OF A PRESSURE CANNER

There are varying levels of trepidation when it comes to pressure canning, and I believe some degree of this worry comes from being unfamiliar with the parts of a pressure canner. I think it will benefit you immensely to learn the parts and what's normal versus what's not while pressure canning.

The lid, which is sometimes called the "cover," has many safety features located on it—which I'll describe directly below—and knowing their names and what they do can help you determine if a thrift store purchase or used pressure canner is a good buy or if you should pass it up.

The pressure dial gauge on top and typically in the center of the lid of a dial-gauge pressure canner is round and has a dial with a needle indicating the pounds or metric units of pressure (depending on the manufacturer) that have been built up inside the pressure canner. This gauge also indicates, indirectly, how much heat is inside.

All pressure canning recipes will indicate the pounds of pressure needed for a particular recipe and for your elevation. This round dial will typically indicate between ten and fifteen pounds of pressure during the canning process, but the display will usually span between zero and twenty pounds of pressure. The dial is a critical part of the safety features in a pressure canner; you cannot safely pressure can without a dial.

The pressure regulator is a safety device, located on top of the vent pipe, which rocks back and forth during the canning process and intermittently releases a little bit of pressure several times a minute, making a "shhhh . . . shhhh . . ." sound. This sound signals to the canner that a little bit of pressure is being released (safely!) as the process continues. It is a round, usually black and silver device that maintains a steady, metronome-like beat; a sort of "heartbeat" of the pressure canning process.

Like a heartbeat, you should take action if the "beat" or "shhhh . . . shhhh" becomes too fast-paced. If a "shhhh" is occurring every one or two seconds, the pressure dial gauge will surely be climbing over fifteen pounds of pressure into dangerous levels of pressure. If this happens, turn off the heat immediately and, if possible, move the pressure canner to a cool burner.

You can always "take your foot off the gas pedal" and turn off the heat during the canning process. Should you reduce the heat significantly while canning, watch the dial, and the canning process can continue uninterrupted *as long as you maintain the minimum pressure during this cooldown period*. If you need to turn the heat off while canning and before the time required has elapsed, and the pressure drops below the required level, cool it all the way to zero pressure, wait until the jars are quite cool, pour all the preserves out into a preserving pan, and start the process over.

The pressure regulator sits atop the next important part of the pressure canner anatomy: the vent pipe. Similar to a wood stove chimney, a vent pipe's steam (instead of smoke) will begin to flow upward from it during the exhaustion process, before you start your processing time. It is this vent pipe, absent its pressure regulator "hat," that you'll watch closely during exhausting. After steam has vented from the vent pipe for ten minutes, you will place the pressure regulator on top of the vent pipe.

It should be noted that the vent pipe has a very narrow opening, and it can become clogged. Before and after every canning session, and after every pressure cooking session especially, review the pipe to see if there is any blockage. Hard water buildup is a likely blockage culprit.

Also, if you had a jar break during the pressure canning process, the food therein could clog it, as well. Clean the entire vent pipe opening with a toothpick, pipe cleaner, or cleaning brush designed for reusable straws or baby bottle nipples. The vent pipe should not be dented or bent, either—check that part thoroughly in advance of purchasing a pressure canner, if you're shopping for a used pressure canner.

My mentor when I was a new English teacher was also my high school chemistry teacher, a very smart and kind man named Mr. McGonigal. He once told me an instructive anecdote about the dangers of a clogged pressure canner/cooker vent pipe, and it begs to be retold to you now.

In a cooking endeavor fueled by the modest budget of a newlywed duo, he and his wife were pressure cooking the ever-thrifty pinto bean to later be canned, ready to eat. The vent pipe became plugged, perhaps by a bean skin. Mr. McGonigal knew there was trouble afoot because the weighted gauge stopped rocking. Remember, the weighted gauge normally rocks gently, intermittently releasing a bit of steam to help maintain proper pressure inside, for both cooking and canning.

He took the pot off the heat (which was smart on his part) and immediately removed the weight. With the weighted gauge removed, an Old Faithful–esque plume of steam and beans shot upward to the ceiling, frightening everyone and creating a huge mess!

What's the moral of this story? Ensuring the tiny vent pipe's opening is clean, free, and clear is critical for safely releasing little spurts of pressure all throughout the canning process. *This* is what Mr. McGonigal affirmed, and what you'll be reminded of in this book, so that your pressure canning experience will be enjoyable *and* safe, just the way it's meant to be!

One last reminder: It's very important with any pressure canner that the vent pipe remains unblocked. Should you ever find yourself observing signs from the many safety features on your pressure canner that there *is* a blockage (or trouble of any sort), the best course of action is to turn off the heat immediately.

Let's see, what's next? The canning rack is placed in the bottom of the canner. And the fact is, all canners should come with a rack that fits nicely in the bottom. Without it, your jars will rattle around like crazy and very likely break. (So, if you're buying a thrift store pressure canner or a used one from anywhere at all, check to see that the rack sits perfectly flat and without wiggle in the bottom. If it doesn't, don't buy it, or be prepared to purchase a rack separately!)

The pressure canner's rack allows water to flow all the way around the jars, heating the contents thoroughly. In a pressure canner, you can place an additional rack (either another pressure canner rack or a similarly sized cooling rack) directly on top of your filled jars in order to create a bunk bed of jars inside the pressure canner. This allows for more jars to be processed in the same batch. The canning rack should be free from rust, so take note of the finish of a used rack before purchasing.

The air vent, sometimes called a cover lock, is a small, silver apparatus that pops up and away from the surface of the lid when sufficient pressure has been built up inside. This safety feature shows you visually that there's pressure inside and therefore you should *not* open the lid.

As the pressure drops when the canning process is completed, the air vent/cover lock will slowly become flush with the lid once more, as it was before you began the canning process. This indicates there is no more pressure inside and that it is safe to open the lid.

The overpressure plug is a black, rubber, button-sized plug on the surface of the pressure canner lid. If it were separate from the lid, it would resemble a cartoon mushroom. It will pop out of the lid automatically and release steam in the event that the vent pipe becomes plugged and/or pressure cannot be released normally.

If the overpressure plug pops out during the pressure canning process, this should signal to you a near-emergency situation and you should immediately turn the heat off and move the pressure canner off the burner, if possible.

Upon examining a used pressure canner, if you find this plug is brittle, cracked, aged, or missing, look up the manufacturer of the pressure canner and determine if a new plug is available before purchasing. Many manufacturers offer these as inexpensive, readily available replacement parts. However, if you *cannot* find a replacement for the overpressure plug, I would not buy or use that particular pressure canner.

The advantage of purchasing a new canner is it will be sure to have all the safety features available, and those parts will be in good working order. In particular, the gasket and rubber overpressure plug will not have degraded over time. Of course, getting a new pressure canner comes at an expense. If you buy a used canner, though, be sure to review this book's list of parts and decide if there are as many or nearly as many safety features as on a new pressure canner.

Also, keep in mind the time and cost of purchasing replacement parts, which can vary from quick and affordable to time-consuming and expensive; and let these factors guide your decision in purchasing the perfect pressure canner for you.

It may be very tempting to use a very old pressure canner, especially if a loved one used it, too, years ago. I am as sentimental as they come, so I understand the desire to honor our loved ones, those industrious matriarchs and patriarchs who were so tough and hardworking. But if the old pressure canner in question doesn't have replacement parts available, you can't figure out what make or model it is, it has dents, rust, or is otherwise compromised, I would bet the original owner wouldn't want you to get hurt using it. They'd likely want you to preserve effectively, quickly, and safely! Save an old canner for sentiment if you wish, but use one for pressure canning with working parts and as many safety features as possible. (An old canner can be used to store lids and rings, be displayed with handwritten recipe cards or bouquets of flowers, and more!) The bottom line is purchase and use the best, safest canner you're able to get.

There's one last heartfelt sentiment I'd like to share with you here. Old recipes are touchstones to our past and are links to the women and men who inspire us to preserve today. The handwritten recipe cards in your family's canon can be identified immediately by handwriting, card style, and recipe type. They are portals to the past that help us recall memories from our childhood (see Gram's Hamburger Soup recipe on page 91 for a peek into my childhood recipe tradition).

You can review old recipes (that is, anything older than twenty-five years) and stay true to their spirit and flavor by comparing those recipes to ones in this book. If a recipe is very similar in ingredients and proportions (for example, similar ratios of vegetables to meat), pressure can them using the times listed in this book or in other trusted canning literature. Use the times listed for the longest-processing ingredients. For example, if you have vegetables and meat in a recipe, use the times for processing meat, since meat has a longer processing time than most vegetables. If your old recipes have ingredients that are not safe for pressure canning (dairy or grains, in particular), omit them, of course; *but* I encourage you to pressure can the recipe "base" (like a soup base!), then later add those grains or dairy products when you reheat the jars, ready to eat.

Chapter 4

LET THE FUN BEGIN! HERE'S HOW TO PRESSURE CAN

Once you've selected a pressure canning recipe at least a day in advance, prepared and cooked the recipe as required, *and* you have at least two hours ahead of you where you'll be unrushed and available to stay at home, near or in the kitchen, you're then ready to pressure can.

First, look over your pressure canner to make sure your lid and the pressure regulator that goes over the vent pipe are present and unbroken, and you have a rack that sits nicely in the bottom of the canner. The canner should be clean inside and out.

Then, center the pressure canner on your stovetop burner, considering its proximity to the countertop. I always place mine as far back as possible because I have young kids and I don't want any fingertips near the hot canner.

Next, fill the jars you plan to fill with preserves with very hot tap water or water from a tea kettle. Place them next to the stove or sink (preferably, if such a location exists, near both) on a towel-covered countertop. The heat from the water heats the glass jars nicely and the towel insulates the hot jars from a potentially cold countertop. A towel also protects them from thermal shock, which can cause a hot jar to break.

Once the jars have been heated up by the hot water, pour the water down the sink drain one jar at a time. This way, each jar will first be warming up with hot water, then, after emptying it of the warming hot water, you'll refill each with your broth, soup, meat, etc., put the lid on, and set it in the pressure canner. This procedure keeps the jars

appropriately warm while you're cooking your preserve, and while you're filling the other jars.

Start by checking your manufacturer's directions for how many quarts of water to put in the bottom of your pressure canner. Typically, it's between two to four quarts. This amount is often confused or misquoted with the number of inches that are in the bottom of the canner. Three quarts of water *may* be three inches in the bottom, but it may not. Refer to the manufacturer's manual for the exact amount of water required. FYI, I use hot tap water to fill the pot. I also suggest adding a splash of vinegar (a quarter cup is plenty) to the pot if your water is hard. This will prevent the minerals in the water from forming a white film on the jars *and* from clogging the vent pipe. (My water is so hard, if I forget the vinegar when canning, my jars look like they have a skiff of snow on them!) Place the canner—with the rack on the bottom and the required amount of water in it—onto the stove and turn it on low. This step of preheating the water is done in the name of preventing jars from breaking from thermal shock.

Important note: The recipes you'll be pressure canning will either be "hot pack" (more on this later, but hot pack includes the foods you'll be preserving that are pre-cooked or otherwise hot, like in the Mexican Bean and Bone recipe on page 116) or "raw pack" (that is, when the ingredients you'll be preserving are uncooked, like in the Fish Taco Tilapia recipe on page 129). For a hot pack recipe, the water in the bottom of the pressure canner needs to be heated to 180°F. For a raw pack recipe, the water in the bottom of the pressure canner only needs to be heated to 140°F.

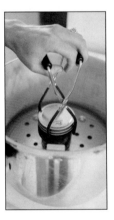

Now, dump one jar's hot water out into the sink. Using a funnel and ladle, add the preserve (soup, stew, beans, vegetables, broth, meat, etc.) to the jar, being sure to maintain proper headspace (the distance between the top of the food and the top of the jar, indicated in the recipe, typically between an inch and an inch and a half). Add a new lid and ring and tighten it fingertip tight. This means only as tight as you'd tighten a faucet. You do *not* want it overtightened, as that *can* cause a lid to buckle. You also want oxygen to be able to escape during the processing time.

Using a jar lifter, place the filled and lidded jar into the warm water in the pressure canner (remember, the contents of the jar are likely very hot!). Repeat this process until the canner is filled with filled jars or until you run out of preserves. Jars should not be touching. Keep the jars upright; do not allow the food in them to slosh around, since that can compromise your seal. Jars *can* be stacked, if you use a rack specifically for this purpose, i.e., one that allows steam to flow all the way around the jars. Do *not* stack jars directly atop one another.

Place the lid on the pressure canner according to the manufacturer's directions. The lid should be locked firmly in place, likely by screwing or twisting either the lid itself or screws along the edge of the lid. Turn the heat on the stove to medium and be sure the weight is off the vent port and set aside, or if your model of canner has one, the petcock (pressure regulator) is *open*.

As the canner warms, not much will visibly happen. This is normal. In a few minutes, depending on your stove and canner, a vent of steam will become visible through the port, which, as a reminder, is a little "chimney" sticking up less than an inch tall from

the surface of the pressure canner lid. From this chimney steam will soon pour. Start the timer for the amount of time indicated on your manufacturer's directions, typically ten minutes. *This critical step, called exhausting or venting, fills the canner with pure steam.* In my pressure canner, for example, and with most canners, it's required to let ten minutes of continuous steam flow out of the vent. After ten minutes (or other time indicated in your manual), place the weight on top of the port or close the petcock.

Now, pressure will begin to build inside the canner and the many safety features of your pressure canner (if it's a newer model) will start their work. There's the metal vent lock that will, in perhaps five minutes, pop up out of the lid indicating that pressure is beginning to build inside the pressure canner. Then, the dial on the gauge will start to climb. All recipes have a specific number of pounds of pressure required for safe processing. When the dial climbs to between ten to fifteen pounds of pressure, the heat can be reduced to medium or medium low. Turn it to medium if you are right at or a few pounds *above* the target pressure, or turn it to low if you are significantly far above the target pressure. This adjustment to your stove should maintain the appropriate pressure for the duration of the processing time.

Once the appropriate pressure is reached for your particular recipe and elevation, you may start the processing timer. (Remember, above sea level you'll be required to add pounds of pressure. The chart for adjustment to pounds of pressure for elevation can be found on page 33.)

Another important note: The rubber plug should not move and nothing will happen with it *during a safe canning process*. Why? Because it's a safety valve for releasing pressure in the instance of too much pressure buildup.

In all my years of pressure canning, I've found some liquids only require a processing time of twenty-five minutes—for example, Basic Bone Broth (page 35). However, many thicker or meatier recipes call for up to ninety minutes of processing time (see the Chicken with Potatoes and Garlic recipe on page 106). For the first several times you pressure can, I strongly suggest you stay in the kitchen or very nearby to monitor the dial or gauge, in order to maintain appropriate pressure for the duration of the processing time.

On my electric coil stove, the heat and accompanying pressure is very stable. Once my canner is up to pressure, I lower the temperature to medium-low (a "3" on my dial, out of "8") and it maintains itself right at the required eleven pounds of pressure for my elevation. The pressure remains stable for the processing time in this way, never needing adjustment. Your stove may be different, meaning you may need to turn your electric coil stove to a higher temperature than medium-low to reach and sustain the required number of pounds of pressure for your elevation. If you have a gas stove, your temperature dial may necessitate you turning it higher or lower than medium-low to reach and sustain the required number of pounds of pressure for your elevation.

Once the processing time has elapsed, turn off the stove. *Do not do anything*. Let the pressure canner cool. Opening the canner too early is an excellent way to hurt yourself. An incredible amount of pressure has built up inside; the worst thing you could do is open the canner before pressure has slowly decreased naturally.

Side note: You actually *could* leave jars inside the locked pressure canner for twelve hours, if that made you feel safer! That's not necessary, of course, but you could wait that long if it would ease your mind. The quality of the food you're preserving won't suffer if you let it cool in the pressure canner. *The pressure canner's lid is safe to open when the metal vent lock is down, the lid is cooler to the touch (you could comfortably touch it with a bare hand), and the dial reads zero pounds of pressure within the canner.* The dial reading is very important, and another reason to ensure the dial is reading pressure accurately. When I'm pressure canning, I usually turn the heat off at the end of the processing time and do something else for an hour or two. Then, when I return, everything is quite cool and there's no question that it's safe to open the lid.

Open the lid away from yourself, remove the jars, and place them onto a towel-covered countertop. The contents of the jar will bubble—sometimes for a few hours—after being removed; this is normal. Do not disturb the jars and do not press down on the lids to force them to seal. Once cooled completely (typically twenty-four hours later), remove the rings, wipe the outside of the jars with a warm, damp cloth to remove any food debris, then label and store them in a cool, dark place. A pantry shelf is ideal, as is a cellar, basement, or cupboard shelf. Remember that light will degrade the appearance and texture of foods, so a sunny shelf won't immediately make your preserves unsafe, but it will make them look unappetizing sooner than if stored out of direct light.

If you have a jar that didn't seal, you can simply refrigerate it and eat it as you would normally, with a normal sense about its expiration date (i.e., without a proper seal, it's now *not* considered canned or preserved, so be smart and safe about consuming it sooner than later).

You may find several jars that didn't seal. The most common cause is too great an increase or decrease in temperature during the canning process. If this occurs, you can remove all the food from the jars, bring the food to a boil, and re-can everything using new lids. However, be sure to increase the temperature more gradually next time. Rapid increase in temperature can cause siphoning, which is the food inside the jars bubbling out of the jar, inhibiting seal formation. Too rapid a decrease in temperature can be caused by turning off the heat to the pressure canner and cranking the air conditioning or otherwise allowing the kitchen to cool dramatically. I've never had this luxury and thus have never felt like my jars experienced this (though I certainly have turned on a fan and wanted my kitchen to cool down as soon as possible). So, don't worry too much about too rapid a decrease, as it isn't likely to occur without a significant swing in temperature. The important takeaway here is *gradual* temperature changes are best when canning. Raise and lower the temperature slowly and gradually, in order to can more quickly and effectively. On that note, more pounds of pressure, that is, more heat, is not better. There's no advantage to heating the pressure canner so the pressure therein is above fifteen pounds; in fact, that's a dangerous idea altogether. More is not better, in this case.

Now, there are a number of exceptions to this next statement, so understand that each recipe is unique. When pressure canning, you have the option between raw packing or hot packing foods. At a glance, it seems faster, easier, and thus better to pack jars with raw (that is, uncooked, cold, or room temperature) ingredients. However, generally, a much more delicious, fragrant, aesthetically pleasing result is achieved by hot packing.

Hot packing entails cooking, browning, or otherwise preparing with heat the recipe in question before it is poured into jars and pressure canned. Browned meats taste better than raw packed meat. Presoaked beans cooked into soups and stews are dynamite when pressure canned. Taking the time to precook meats and vegetables and presoak beans makes the final result dramatically better in many recipes.

In this book, I'll give directions for how to produce the *tastiest* jars. If pressure canning friends mention that you *could* just raw pack, it's good to know you could, but normally you won't want to, in order to get the most delicious results.

How this plays out in *my* kitchen is I soak beans, buy meat, or take meat out of the freezer on day one. That same day, I may chop veggies and store them in a container in the fridge, if the recipe calls for them. The following day, I brown the meat, assemble the vegetables, season, then pressure can most of the recipe, except the amount my family will eat fresh that evening for supper. Indeed, I canned this way for months while writing this book. The factors that largely dictated what recipes I tested and when were: what my family wanted for supper, the weather, and the "fresh ingredient availability" at the time. You can absolutely can half a recipe and eat the remainder fresh from many recipes in this book. There's no reason to fill the pressure canner with jars and, in fact, you could pressure can a single jar if you wanted to. Pressure canners operate just as safely with the maximum number of jars as they do with a single jar. Or double the recipe provided and can a full batch and eat fresh or freeze the remaining.

FILLING THE CANNER

You do not have to fill the canner full of jars in order to safely process. That is, you can safely process a single jar. If you want to stack jars and can two layers at once, use a metal canning rack—which you'll place on top of the first layer of jars—and just be sure all the bottom layer of jars are the same height. Before you begin the canning process, test out the layering with cold, empty jars with lids and rings on, in order to see exactly how much room you have. If your layers of jars will comfortably fit inside with the lid on, you're good to go. (Note: This is *not* something to figure out with hot jars filled with boiling hot preserves.)

Of course, you *could* pressure can *two* batches in a day. (Many an industrious canner has canned several batches a day or had more than one pressure canner on the stove at a time.) After you've done the process of pressure canning once or twice, it will become very natural to start thinking, *What should I make for tomorrow's supper?* instead of *What should I make for supper in an hour?* You'll be amazed at how handy it is to meal prep shelf-stable meals in this way.

Another option to consider: You can also use different sizes of jars to further assist in meal preparation: pints are perfect for a hearty lunch for one, and half pints are an ideal size for a child or elderly person. (I try to always can a few half pints of recipes for my grandmother, given she lives alone, and I want her to have an easy little meal available when she doesn't feel like cooking). Of course, quarts are ideal for versatile broth-based soups for a small family. Note that many recipes do not offer a processing time for quart jars; this is because a smaller-sized jar (pint, or about two cups) is what is required for heat to penetrate the ingredients to an appropriate level. You can always can in a smaller jar, but do *not* can in a larger one, if no time is provided for such in the recipe you're considering.

HOW TO GET COMFORTABLE PRESSURE CANNING

Some readers will dive in, choosing a hearty chili (see recipes on page 89) or soup (see recipes on page 31) and never look back. For the more hesitant new canner, I completely understand. My husband didn't ease my worries when I started, unhelpfully noting how the pressure regulator's rhythmic "shhhh . . . shhhh . . . shhhh . . ." sounded like a ticking bomb! Now I hear that sound and know I'm right on track, but I was of course nervous the first several batches I canned with my pressure canner.

Here are my best tips for getting comfortable with the pressure canning process.

1. Learn the parts of the pressure canner and memorize their names. (Yes, this may sound like "homework," but I promise you by following through with it, you'll feel much more comfortable with pressure canning!) Before you even try the canning process, label each part with a sticky note and leave the notes where you can see them and review them several times a day. Reading this book, your pressure canner's manufacturer's manual, and any other tested recipe will make more sense to you, *and* you'll feel more confident if you know the names of the parts referenced. You *could* also write the names of the vent port, overpressure plug, etc. directly on the lid of your canner with a permanent marker. You won't be able to label every part this way, but you would for several of them and you'd have a permanent label to reference. I'm encouraging you to learn the difference between each part, know what they do, and why they're important, so that you'll feel much better going forward.

2. Read the manufacturer's manual that came with the pressure canner or find it online. Pressure canner companies have very good resources on their websites for accessing (and downloading and printing) various models of pressure canner manuals and guides. I purchased my Presto pressure canner new but misplaced the manual after a few seasons. It was surprisingly easy to find the exact manual I needed on their website. Manufacturers also have excellent resources on their YouTube channels. If you have thrifted or been given a used pressure canner and you cannot determine by the markings on it the make and/or model, or you cannot find a manual online or elsewhere, I would suggest using another pressure canner. (Yes, it's that important!) However, resources for finding a manual also include your local cooperative extension office or library. The fact is, your manual will tell you, among other things, how much water is required in the bottom of the pot at the beginning of the pressure canning process, and this amount is essential to get right. Do your due diligence and read the correct manual for the canner you intend to use, and you'll feel much more assured.

3. Practice by canning water. You'll read the "recipe" for pressure canning water on page 32, but it's as simple as you imagine. Canning water allows you to go through the steps of filling the jars, filling

the canner with the proper amount of water, exhausting it, placing the pressure regulator on the vent pipe, watching the dial climb or the rocking dial begin to rock, and finally, setting your timer for the required time. You'll also get to practice allowing the canner to cool, *and* you'll feel the satisfaction of hearing the lids ping or testing them with your finger to determine when they're sufficiently cool. Besides, *everyone* could use canned water for emergency preparedness, and it's a great practice step that will build your confidence (and stock your emergency kit).

4. Pressure can a recipe with a few simple ingredients. I suggest the Mighty Flavorful Mushrooms recipe (page 44) because it's comprised simply of mushrooms and some herbs. It's also a high "wow factor" recipe, because the mushrooms are appetizer-plate ready, giftable, and delicious. This small-batch recipe only calls for a few jars and is quick to prepare, making it ideal for a beginner.

5. I suggest making the same recipe a few times in a row and within a few days of one another. Pressure canning once a year (like I used to!) doesn't really allow you to become comfortable with the process. Plan ahead to make a run of it and use your pressure canner a few times during a single week or even over a weekend.

6. Meal plan with pressure canning in mind. This prevents you from having to prepare two recipes and creates time for you to preserve during an otherwise busy day. Carving out the time to practice any new skill is half the battle in learning it, right?

7. Ask for help if you need it. I recommend reaching out to a local (or even far away, since you can always call or email them!) cooperative extension office, if you have questions. Their experts will guide you with tested, trusted information for when you're uncertain.

8. Any time you refer to a search engine like Google, include the search terms, "+ cooperative extension" so the recipes or instructions you find are sure to be high quality information. By using these search terms, you'll avoid a glut of bad advice and get solid information, enhancing and bolstering your confidence. Furthermore, you'll notice the same guidelines and advice repeated across cooperative extension offices; that is, you won't have the variability of self-taught "experts" sharing their anecdotal stories. You'll be provided with the same science-backed recommendations and instructions, over and over.

PART II

Chapter 5
PRESSURE CANNING RECIPES

Basic Broths and Stocks

In Part II of this book, you'll find several different recipe sections. First, you'll find the basics, which are the fastest to prepare of all the recipes I'll be sharing with you herein. Keep in mind that, generally, the more liquid in a preserve, the shorter the preserving time will be. Broth processes more quickly than a stew, and chunks of meat tend to process the longest. In this basics section, you'll find versatile broths, including the "superhero" bone broth with expanded instructions on how to craft and customize this pantry essential.

Then, you'll find recipes for what are, at the heart of it, simple jars of either veggies or meat. Some of you will live and dwell in this section, filling your pantry shelves with jars of recipe building blocks that make your grocery store tin-can counterparts pale in comparison!

Beyond the basics are meals in jars. You'll get recipes for truly hearty preserved meals that you'll have ready for lunch in the car, a supper at a sports practice, or a healthy bite at the office. (Think meat and potatoes, beans and vegetables, and meals that will fill you up *and* tickle your taste buds.)

One final note: You'll very likely notice that every recipe ends with the exact same process (with some minor variations to account for the type of food, number of pounds of pressure, and length of time processing). This is because each recipe *does* require these same steps *and* it's the simplest, most effective way to convey it to you. (I believe you'll also absorb and store this information more readily through its repetition.)

PLAIN WATER

YIELD: 7 QUARTS

Canning water is a great first foray into using your pressure canner. Jars of canned water, by the way, can be stored indefinitely for use during an extended power outage or emergency. I grew up with jars of water under every sink in our house, for use during a potential (nay, inevitable) electrical outage. If you intend to save this water for human consumption, use the purest water available. For most of us, this would be tap water. For those preserving well water, it would be best to filter out any minerals or organic matter present before pressure canning. This recipe could merely be a means to practice using your pressure canner, but these jars could also be a practical "gift" as an addition to any emergency preparedness kit for a loved one or friend.

YOU WILL NEED

7 quarts water

1. Prepare your pressure canner. Fill the pot with hot water in the amount specified by the manufacturer (2 to 3 quarts is typical). Warm your jars by filling them with hot tap water and placing them near your cooking area. Prepare your rings and new lids by placing them in pairs (one new lid nested with one clean ring) nearby.

2. Turn on the burner, the one on which the canner is sitting, to warm. Fill each jar with hot water, maintaining 1 inch of head space. Apply new lids and rings fingertip tight to each jar and place on the rack at the bottom of the pressure canner. Place the pressure canner lid on and secure according to the manufacturer's directions. Increase the heat to medium and exhaust per the manufacturer's directions (typically for 10 minutes). Process at 11 pounds of pressure at sea level for 10 minutes for pints or quarts. When the time is up, turn the burner off and do *nothing* until the pressure valve on your pressure canner lid is completely released/flush with the lid and the dial indicates 0 pounds of pressure.

NOTE: Pressure canning accidents occur when a canner opens the lid before the pressure has been released. You cannot rush this step. I recommend leaving the canner for a few hours to cool down completely.

IN A DIAL GAUGE PRESSURE CANNER

At elevations of 0–2,000 feet, process at **11** pounds pressure

At elevations of 2,001–4,000 feet, process at **12** pounds pressure

At elevations of 4,001–6,000 feet, process at **13** pounds pressure

At elevations of 6,001–8,000 feet, process at **14** pounds pressure

At elevations of 8,001–10,000 feet, process at **15** pounds pressure

IN A WEIGHTED GAUGE PRESSURE CANNER

At elevations of 0–1,000 feet, process at **10** pounds pressure

At elevations 1,001 feet and above, process at **15** pounds pressure

BASIC BONE BROTH

YIELD: DEPENDENT UPON QUANTITY OF RAW INGREDIENTS (1 TRAY OF BONES WILL YIELD AT LEAST 7 QUARTS)

Bone broth is all the rage, for good reason. Aside from the powerful dose of nutrition it provides, it makes everything you cook in it far more flavorful and delicious. It's the secret ingredient to many dishes that gives depth and richness you can't get any other way. This is the recipe that, once you make it, you can't can enough! Truly, there may not be a more useful staple. Golden, rich, and gelatinous, bone broth is different from "normal" broth, in that it's teeming with the goodness from roasted and simmered bones and has been simmered down to be even richer. So, there's less water and more goodness! The best bone broth I've made has been with venison bones, which I know aren't readily available to many, except those belonging to hunting households. If you have access to them, they make excellent bone broth and I prefer them even to beef bones . . . and that's saying a lot coming from a rancher's daughter! It's best to begin the bone broth process a few days before canning will commence, as there are several simple but time-consuming steps involved: roasting, simmering, straining, and finally, pressure canning.

YOU WILL NEED

Bones: Enough beef, venison, chicken, or other to fill your largest baking sheet in a single layer. For bulkier beef bones, this will be several (up to 10 or more!) pounds, but for lighter chicken bones, which are thinner, it will be fewer. You can (and perhaps should) include chicken feet, carefully cleaned, as well. Bones can (and ideally do, in fact) have meaty bits left on them. The largest bones should be cracked with a mallet or hammer before roasting. When shopping for bones, some of the best kinds are knuckles, joints, tail, marrow bones, or veal bones (especially prized for bone broth, because of their large amount of cartilage). Any bones will work, however, and will eventually result in a great broth. Don't be shy asking your butcher to cut the bones into 2- to 4-inch sections for you; you want that inner goodness to be readily released, and you'll need all the pieces to fit into your stockpot comfortably. There's no advantage to leaving bones in giant pieces, other than teasing the kids in your household that you're using dinosaur bones!

Aromatic vegetables:
1–2 large carrots
1–2 stalks celery
1–2 onions
2–3 cloves garlic

Assorted herbs:
2–3 bay leaves
1–2 sprigs rosemary
1–2 sprigs oregano
1–2 sprigs thyme

Optional add-ins:
2–3 tablespoons turmeric
2–3 tablespoons dried ginger
1–2 cups apple cider vinegar per batch (especially useful for breaking down and releasing goodness within connective tissue)
1–2 tablespoons peppercorns

(Continued on next page)

NOTE: These optional add-ins can be added, instead, to the individual jars as you ladle the finished broth in, just before processing. This method allows for customization of each jar, whether you want to test out flavors before seasoning a whole batch or create a personalized jar for a friend. Consider this customization technique, as well, if you have a group of friends over for a bone broth party. Invite friends to help with the process and let each friend add their own add-ins just before processing. To speed up the simmering process, consider using an Instant Pot–style appliance, described below.

1. Arrange the bones, aromatic vegetables, and assorted herbs on a baking sheet (and use two baking sheets, if needed, to avoid crowding). Roast at 450°F until browned well (about an hour), stirring at about 30 minutes in.

2. Place the roasted bones, vegetables, and any of the optional add-ins into a stockpot (or two). Cover with water and simmer on low. How long you simmer is determined by a variety of factors. I feel safe keeping my stockpot on the lowest temperature overnight. Instead, you could keep your stockpot on simmer for most of the day. You could also cook the bones and vegetables in a slow cooker for many hours, though many slow cookers are limited by their capacity. You may have to add more water to cover the bones as you simmer, and that is acceptable. Your goal is to cook broth that's rich in color and flavor, and that can take many hours. I always cook my bone broth with a lid on, but slightly askew, so some steam can escape. Alternatively, you can use an Instant Pot–style pressure cooker to speed up the process. If you choose this option, cook for around 2 hours to replicate the hours and hours of simmering. The only thing you'll miss is the heavenly smell wafting through the house all day.

3. Once you've cooked a flavorful, colorful broth, you can remove it from the heat and strain. This alone can be quite a chore; I usually wait till it cools significantly before I pull the bones out. A metal mesh strainer is an ideal way to strain the solids. The vegetables will be very, very soft. A great use for the carrots is to be mashed into baby food or added to a meal at the end of the cooking time. They'll be bursting with goodness. However, these ingredients may be too soft for your liking and can be composted or fed to lucky barnyard chickens, if you or someone you know has them.

4. An important step is to cool the broth so that all the fat solidifies at the top of the broth's surface. This fat is flavorful, nutritious, *and not appropriate for canning*. Save it by removing and storing it in the refrigerator. (Sometimes it's softer and thus scoopable, while other times it's thinner and more like a sheet of ice on a pond, which can be lifted out, in a perfect stockpot-sized circle.) I like to melt this fat later and coat chopped yellow potatoes in it, roasting them at 425°F with garlic salt. Trust me, it results in the best roasted potatoes you've ever made. Do *not* skip removing the solidified fats from the bone broth, as fat will climb the sides of your jar during the pressure canning process and compromise the seal. Fat is delicious, but it has no place in your canning jars.

5. Prepare your pressure canner. Fill the pot with hot water in the amount specified by the manufacturer (2 to 3 quarts is typical). Warm your jars by filling them with hot tap water and placing them near your cooking area. Prepare your rings and new lids by placing them in pairs (one new lid nested with one clean ring) nearby. Assemble the funnel and ladle, as well, and place a kitchen towel on the countertop next to the pressure canner.

6. Turn on the burner, the one on which the canner is sitting, to warm. Pour out the hot water from one jar. Ladle hot bone broth into the jar, leaving 1 inch of headspace. Apply new lids and rings fingertip tight to the jar and place it on the rack at the bottom of the pressure canner. Repeat the same procedure for each jar. Then, place the pressure canner lid on and secure according to the manufacturer's directions. Increase the heat to medium, and exhaust per the manufacturer's directions (typically for 10 minutes). Process at 11 pounds of pressure for 20 minutes for pint jars and 25 minutes for quart jars. When the time is up, turn the burner off and do *nothing* until the pressure valve on your pressure canner lid is completely released/flush with the lid and the dial indicates 0 pounds of pressure.

SEASONINGS ARE THE SPICE OF LIFE!

Some seasonings work well with pressure canning, while others can't stand the heat, *literally*. Fresh herbs are wonderful in many culinary applications, but typically not in pressure canning. The extended heat tends to make for slimy, rather than flavorful herbs. Better options include dried or dehydrated herbs and ground spices. Sage is one herb, however, that experiences a change in flavor when canned. Skip it (even in sausage recipes) to avoid a bitter "off" taste. While onions and garlic have to be used carefully according to tested recipes in water-bath canning—since they're low-acid foods—these rock-star ingredients can be used with abandon in pressure canning. Add all the garlic and onion you want. And remember, precooking (also known as hot packing) can give the best flavor and texture of all when pressure canning.

BONE BROTH WITH A MEDITERRANEAN TWIST

Add 4 to 5 whole tomatoes and ¼ cup balsamic vinegar (which, as a bonus, breaks down connective tissue, further releasing nutrition from the bones) to the simmering stage of the above recipe and prepare identically. Use it as you normally would, but I think you'll love the difference in flavor this modification brings to your jars of tasty bone broth.

BONE BROTH WITH VEGETABLES AND/OR POTATOES

YIELD: 7 QUARTS

Another variation of the Basic Bone Broth recipe (page 35) is to add raw veggies to the broth before canning, but after the broth has been created. The result is a delicious vegetable soup that can be eaten alone or added to a freshly prepared soup or stew. Adding cubes of white or red potatoes are safe but require a longer process time.

YOU WILL NEED

Beets, peeled and cut into 1-inch chunks

Carrots, peeled and cut into 1-inch chunks

Mushrooms, cut into 1-inch chunks

Peppers, cut into 1-inch chunks

Corn (whole kernel)

Optional: white and/or red potatoes, peeled and cubed

1. Fill your jars with the veggies, pour Basic Bone Broth (page 35) on top, and process at 11 pounds of pressure for 30 minutes for pints and 35 minutes for quarts. If adding potatoes, add potatoes to jars with other veggies as described above or on their own and process at 11 pounds of pressure for 35 minutes in pints and 40 minutes in quarts.

THE IMPORTANCE OF PEELING VEGETABLES

Peeling root vegetables is recommended because of the presence of the botulism-spawning bacteria, C. botulinum, on potatoes, carrots, and other root vegetables. When cooking normally, there's no concern at all about this presence; but in pressure canning, it's wise to remove the peels or skins of potatoes, beets, carrots, etc. as a safety precaution. You don't want C. botulinum in your jars if you can help it, and removing the skins does exactly that. These steps take a little extra time but are a safeguard against a mistake in the processing time or failure in the canner. Removing skins removes the potential risk of contracting botulism.

HEALTH BENEFITS OF BONE BROTH

I want to mention there are *many* potential health benefits to consuming bone broth. It can promote good digestive health and joint mobility. The collagen is visible when the bone broth is cooled; the jiggly, Jell-O-like quality of the cooled broth is due to the collagen present. And it turns out collagen contains many important amino acids that contribute to a healthy inflammatory response and healthy aging, as well as skin, nail, and hair health. Indeed, the number of compounds in bone broth reads like the back of an expensive health supplement or a luxury skin-care product ingredient list.

Bone broth is so nutrient-dense and mild on the stomach that many choose to break a fast with it. Consuming or cooking with bone broth gives a huge boost to the flavor of your home-cooked meals, which has a secondary effect on improving health. Delicious food you prepare at home is often more healthful—not to mention less expensive—than store-bought or that from a restaurant. Reserve a jar or two of homemade, pressure canned bone broth for when you or a loved one is feeling sick. Warm up a cup and sip its rich contents. It may not cure what ails you, but it's nourishing and easy on the stomach. Think of bone broth as a supercharged, modern chicken noodle soup.

COOKING WITH BONE BROTH

You can take rice, quinoa, and other grains, and cook them in bone broth, instead of plain water (either straight bone broth or cut with water) and pack all that flavor and nutrition into a different meal altogether. (Goodbye, boring rice and other grains!) Cooking with bone broth makes those humble grains superstars when used for salads or side dishes, marrying their inherent flavor with the broth well. Crack open a jar (or use leftover broth from another recipe), cook your grains in it, and be amazed!

A WORD ABOUT HOW MUCH BONE BROTH TO PRESERVE

At some point you'll wonder how much bone broth you should preserve (actually, you'll ask yourself how much of everything you should preserve) and truly, I don't think you can prepare enough bone broth. For many of the recipes in this book, the base is a broth, and if you can use homemade bone broth, the flavor and nutritional value will be truly exceptional. If you cannot use homemade bone broth for many recipe bases, it's okay! I suggest you use the best quality store-bought broth or stock and proceed with confidence. But once you start eating recipes you've prepared with this bone broth recipe, it will be really hard to settle for a less delicious, less virtuous substitute. This note is not to make you feel as if you must spend an entire month preserving nothing but bone broth, but rather to impress upon you how entirely versatile, useful, and delicious it is. When water-bath canning, I always say you can't can enough tomatoes, and when pressure canning, I affirm you can't can enough bone broth.

One last nudge about the benefits of cooking with pressure canned bone broth: Consider that a quart of liquid is often required (if not 2 or 3 quarts) for a single recipe of stew or soup. Sometimes in these cases, when preparing one of the recipes in the following sections, I'll mix bone broth with water in a 1–1 ratio, just to avoid using up all that special broth, and you can do the same. Once you've read through this book, I suggest reflecting on how many of these recipes you'd like to eventually prepare and have on your pantry shelf. Then, figure out how many quarts of bone broth that would require. It takes a lot of time and work to preserve just 4 quarts of bone broth. That time and work is worth it of course, but our time is limited. My point is, begin your preserving practice with the plan in mind that when time allows, you'll add a batch of bone broth to your preservation calendar, because you'll never *not* want it on your shelves!

TOMATO SOUP WITH BONE BROTH

YIELD: 5-6 QUARTS

This simple classic is elevated in both flavor and nutritional value by the addition of bone broth. Please be aware: This recipe is a large one, one of the largest in the book, in part because it's such a useful staple to have on hand, and because tomatoes yield a lot of soup—the whole thing (besides the core and skin) ends up in the pot!

YOU WILL NEED

14 cups fresh tomatoes or 4 (28-ounce) cans whole tomatoes

2 tablespoons olive oil

4 white onions, diced

3 tablespoons minced garlic or more to taste

8 cups Basic Bone Broth (page 35) or best quality beef, venison, or chicken broth

2 bay leaves

1 tablespoon salt

2 teaspoons black pepper

1. If using fresh tomatoes, peel them by bringing a large pot of water to boil, dropping the tomatoes a few at a time into the boiling water for 1 minute, then removing them with a slotted spoon. Place the tomatoes into an ice bath. When cool enough to handle, slip the tomato skins off. Dice and core the peeled tomatoes, saving as much of the juice as possible.

2. Heat the olive oil in a heavy bottomed pot over medium heat. Add the onions and garlic and sauté until soft. Add the broth, tomatoes, bay leaves, salt, and pepper and simmer for 1 hour. Remove the bay leaves. Use an immersion blender or blender to blend the soup until it's smooth.

3. Prepare your pressure canner. Fill the pot with hot water in the amount specified by the manufacturer (2 to 3 quarts is typical). Warm your jars by filling them with hot tap water and placing them near your cooking area. Prepare your rings and new lids by placing them in pairs (one new lid nested with one clean ring) nearby. Assemble the funnel and ladle, as well, and place a kitchen towel on the countertop next to the pressure canner.

4. Turn on the burner, the one on which the canner is sitting, to warm. Pour out the hot water from one jar. Ladle hot soup into the jar, leaving 1 inch of headspace. Apply new lids and rings fingertip tight to the jar and place it on the rack at the bottom of the pressure canner. Repeat the same procedure for each jar. Then, place the pressure canner lid on and secure according to the manufacturer's directions. Increase the heat to medium, and exhaust per the manufacturer's directions (typically for 10 minutes). Process at 11 pounds of pressure for 35 minutes for pint jars and 45 minutes for quart jars. When the time is up, turn the burner off and do *nothing* until the pressure valve on your pressure canner lid is completely released/flush with the lid and the dial indicates 0 pounds of pressure.

VEGETABLE STOCK

YIELD: ABOUT 7 QUARTS

Vegetable stock is another pantry superstar that can be made with a variety of vegetables, leftovers, stragglers, or otherwise, and preparing it can take a lot less time than bone broth. When you cook with this stock, you'll bring rich, wholesome flavor to countless dishes! Preserve it in as great a quantity as you're able, in order to stock your pantry shelves with a versatile and virtuous ingredient.

YOU WILL NEED

6 carrots, tops removed

6 stalks celery (leaves can be left on, but leafy greens will result in a broth that is not as clear)

3 onions, peeled and chopped

3 tomatoes, cored and chopped

1 cup assorted vegetables (peppers, garlic, etc.), chopped

Optional: 1 cup herbs and spices (rosemary, thyme, bay leaves, peppercorns), avoiding very leafy, delicate greens, as they simply don't hold up well

2 teaspoons salt

1. Clean and prepare all vegetables well and place in a large stockpot. Add any herbs and spices you wish. Cover with water (about 16 cups, or as much as the stockpot can accommodate) and simmer, covered, for 2 hours. Cool and strain, then add in the salt.

2. Using a strainer, strain the vegetables from the broth. These veggies make great compost or food for homestead animals. Or, add them to tonight's supper, or mash them for baby food. All are great options.

3. Prepare your pressure canner. Fill the pot with hot water in the amount specified by the manufacturer (2 to 3 quarts is typical). Warm your jars by filling them with hot tap water and placing them near your cooking area. Prepare your rings and new lids by placing them in pairs (one new lid nested with one clean ring) nearby. Assemble the funnel and ladle, as well, and place a kitchen towel on the countertop next to the pressure canner.

4. Turn on the burner, the one on which the canner is sitting, to warm. Pour out the hot water from one jar. Ladle hot vegetable stock into the jar, leaving 1 inch of headspace. Apply new lids and rings fingertip tight to the jar and place it on the rack at the bottom of the pressure canner. Repeat the same procedure for each jar. Then, place the pressure canner lid on and secure according to the manufacturer's directions. Increase the heat to medium, and exhaust per the manufacturer's directions (typically for 10 minutes). Process at 11 pounds of pressure for 30 minutes for pint jars and 35 minutes for quart jars. When the time is up, turn the burner off and do *nothing* until the pressure valve on your pressure canner lid is completely released/flush with the lid and the dial indicates 0 pounds of pressure.

ROASTED MUSHROOM STOCK

YIELD: ABOUT 3 QUARTS

If you crave a rich stock, but don't have access to bones or time to prepare the almighty bone broth, this recipe is the ticket! This is also a great broth for those who abstain from meat, as it gives a rich color (much darker than regular vegetable broth) and delicious flavor. It's one of many recipes in this book that can be prepared in part one day and completed the next. Roasting the veggies, simmering the stock, then pressure canning can happen on separate days or all in sequence in one day.

YOU WILL NEED

2 pounds mixture of white and cremini mushrooms, cleaned and trimmed (note: cremini mushrooms give the broth an especially rich color and flavor, more closely mimicking animal broth)

1 large white onion, diced small

1 pound leeks, dark green parts removed, sliced thin

1 pound carrots, diced small

1 head garlic

2 tablespoons olive oil

2 tablespoons mixed green herbs (marjoram, rosemary, and thyme)

1 tablespoon black peppercorns

1 bay leaf

1. Preheat oven to 375°F. In a bowl, toss the mushrooms, onion, leeks, carrots, and garlic with the olive oil. Spread the vegetables on a baking sheet (avoid crowding) and roast for 1 hour, stirring at the 30-minute mark.

2. Add the roasted vegetables to a stockpot with 4 quarts water, the mixed green herbs, peppercorns, and bay leaf. Simmer for about an hour. The broth is done when the vegetables are very tender. Skim with a spoon any scum that forms on the surface. When the stock has cooled a bit, strain using a fine-mesh strainer. At this point, you have the option of simmering it further (bringing your yield down from 4 quarts to about 3 quarts or even less, depending on how long you cook it). That is the trade-off; richer stock will yield fewer jars. When you're satisfied with the flavor, you are ready to preserve.

3. Prepare your pressure canner. Fill the pot with hot water in the amount specified by the manufacturer (2 to 3 quarts is typical). Warm your jars by filling them with hot tap water and placing them near your cooking area. Prepare your rings and new lids by placing them in pairs (one new lid nested with one clean ring) nearby. Assemble the funnel and ladle, as well, and place a kitchen towel on the countertop next to the pressure canner.

4. Turn on the burner, the one on which the canner is sitting, to warm. Pour out the hot water from one jar. Ladle hot mushroom stock into the jar, leaving 1 inch of headspace. Apply new lids and rings fingertip tight to the jar and place it on the rack at the bottom of the pressure canner. Repeat the same procedure for each jar. Then, place the pressure

canner lid on and secure according to the manufacturer's directions. Increase the heat to medium, and exhaust per the manufacturer's directions (typically for 10 minutes). Process at 11 pounds of pressure for 30 minutes for pint jars and 35 minutes for quart jars. When the time is up, turn the burner off and do *nothing* until the pressure valve on your pressure canner lid is completely released/flush with the lid and the dial indicates 0 pounds of pressure.

MIGHTY FLAVORFUL MUSHROOMS

YIELD: 3 PINTS

These pressure canned mushrooms can be seasoned how you wish by adding red pepper flakes, garlic, herbs, essential oils, and other seasonings. They're a powerful little vehicle of flavor to be added to recipes later, making this recipe an uber valuable pantry staple. These mushrooms are also right at home on a charcuterie plate.

YOU WILL NEED

6 cups firm white button
    mushrooms
½ teaspoon salt per pint jar

**Seasoning options
(amounts are per pint
jar, so multiply by
number of pint jars):**
1 tablespoon chopped
    garlic
and/or
1 drop rosemary or other
    herbal essential oil
and/or
1 sprig rosemary
1 teaspoon black
    peppercorn

1. Trim the bottom ¼-inch off the stems of your white button mushrooms. Soak in cold water for 10 minutes and drain. Cover cleaned and trimmed mushrooms with water in a saucepan and bring to a boil for 5 minutes.

2. While the water comes to a boil, empty your hot jars of warming water and add ½ teaspoon salt and any or all of the seasoning options to each jar.

3. Prepare your pressure canner. Fill the pot with hot water in the amount specified by the manufacturer (2 to 3 quarts is typical). Warm your jars by filling them with hot tap water and placing them near your cooking area. Prepare your rings and new lids by placing them in pairs (one new lid nested with one clean ring) nearby. Assemble the funnel and ladle, as well, and place a kitchen towel on the countertop next to the pressure canner.

4. Turn on the burner, the one on which the canner is sitting, to warm. Pour out the hot water from one jar. Ladle hot mushrooms into the jar, leaving 1 inch of headspace. Apply new lids and rings fingertip tight to the jar and place it on the rack at the bottom of the pressure canner. Repeat the same procedure for each jar. Then, place the pressure canner lid on and secure according to the manufacturer's directions. Increase the heat to medium, and exhaust per the manufacturer's directions (typically for 10 minutes). Process at 11 pounds of pressure for 45 minutes in pint jars. When the time is up, turn the burner off and do *nothing* until the pressure valve on your pressure canner lid is completely released/flush with the lid and the dial indicates 0 pounds of pressure.

ABOUT ESSENTIAL OILS

Essential oils are especially beneficial to the home canner. A few drops of smartly selected, best-quality essential oil to any of the recipes in this book can give a huge flavor punch. Start with just a drop or two, incorporate, and taste. A single drop will replace roughly a teaspoon of the dried herb or powdered spice. This technique is especially valuable when the flavor you crave comes from a leafy green, which when pressure canned will typically result in a gray-green smudge at the bottom of your canning jar. Basil and cilantro, for example, not only turn to sludge in the pressure canning process, but their bright flavor is all but gone, as well. So, as a more effective alternative, simply use a drop or two of basil or cilantro essential oil! Try black pepper essential oil, instead of peppercorns, which tend to add visual interest, but not the punch of flavor you'd expect. Use lime essential oil in a salsa recipe (especially since canned citrus, with marmalade being the exception, typically isn't as brightly flavored or is downright bitter). Add thyme essential oil for pressure canning recipes featuring beef. When preparing your pressure canning recipe, add the essential oils at the last moment, even adding a drop to the individual jars before ladling in your preserve. This helps limit the total time the oils are exposed to high heat. Bottom line? Try using essential oils to bring intense flavor easily to your pressure canning recipes!

FRENCH ONION SOUP

YIELD: 3 QUARTS

This soup is best served ladled into oven-safe bowls with a slice of crusty bread, then layered on top with cheese, Gruyère being best, with Mozzarella or Swiss being fine, too. Broil before serving to melt the cheese . . . and enjoy!

YOU WILL NEED

6 tablespoons butter
4 pounds yellow onions, sliced into flat ¼-inch thick rounds
2 teaspoons sugar
1 cup cooking sherry
3 quarts best quality beef broth or Basic Bone Broth (page 35)
2 teaspoons dried thyme
Salt and pepper to taste

1. Melt the butter in a heavy bottomed pan or cast-iron skillet over medium heat. Add the onions, spreading them out in as thin a layer as possible. (Consider spreading the onions and butter between two pans to speed up this cooking process.) Sprinkle onions with sugar and stir occasionally, cooking until the onions are soft, golden, and starting to caramelize. This will take 45 minutes to 1 hour. Combine the onions into one pot at this time if they were cooking separately. Add the sherry, stock, and broth, and bring to a simmer.

2. Prepare your pressure canner. Fill the pot with hot water in the amount specified by the manufacturer (2 to 3 quarts is typical). Warm your jars by filling them with hot tap water and placing them near your cooking area. Prepare your rings and new lids by placing them in pairs (one new lid nested with one clean ring) nearby. Assemble the funnel and ladle, as well, and place a kitchen towel on the countertop next to the pressure canner.

3. Turn on the burner, the one on which the canner is sitting, to warm. Pour out the hot water from one jar. Ladle hot soup into the jar, leaving 1 inch of headspace. Apply new lids and rings fingertip tight to the jar and place it on the rack at the bottom of the pressure canner. Repeat the same procedure for each jar. Then, place the pressure canner lid on and secure according to the manufacturer's directions. Increase the heat to medium, and exhaust per the manufacturer's directions (typically for 10 minutes). Process at 11 pounds of pressure for 20 minutes for pint jars and 25 minutes for quart jars. When the time is up, turn the burner off and do *nothing* until the pressure valve on your pressure canner lid is completely released/flush with the lid and the dial indicates 0 pounds of pressure.

EVERY BEAN AND VEGETABLE SOUP

YIELD: 3 PINTS

Much like French Onion Soup (page 47), this soup is best accompanied by a crusty slice of bread, maybe buttered, or a grilled cheese sandwich or a toasted English muffin. Dip in and enjoy this hearty soup.

YOU WILL NEED

1 tablespoon olive oil

1 onion, chopped

1 tablespoon fresh or jarred garlic, crushed or chopped

2 cups dry mixed beans of choice, soaked 8 hours or overnight (Note: most bean mixes include pinto, kidney, lima, split pea, small white, yellow, and navy beans)

2 potatoes, peeled and chopped into 1-inch chunks

2 cups fresh tomato, chopped, or homemade or store-bought tomato sauce of choice

2 carrots, peeled and chopped

2 stalks celery, chopped

1 tablespoon salt

4 cups Vegetable Stock (page 41), chicken stock, Basic Bone Broth (page 35), or Plain Water (page 32)

½ cup red wine vinegar

1–2 bay leaves

1 teaspoon black pepper

Optional: 1 cup corn, canned, frozen, or sliced off the cob

Optional: 2–4 drops liquid smoke (for a fun, smoky flavor)

1. Add the olive oil to your cooking pot and bring to medium heat. Cook the onion and garlic until translucent and a bit browned, then add in all other ingredients. Cook for as long as 2 hours or until the beans are almost as soft as you'd like to eat. They will of course continue to cook during the processing time, but the one batch I didn't cook long enough impressed upon me how disappointing it was to have undercooked beans. No one wants that, so cook it a couple of hours before processing. Note: These steps could be completed before canning, and canning could be done the following day.

2. Prepare your pressure canner. Fill the pot with hot water in the amount specified by the manufacturer (2 to 3 quarts is typical). Warm your jars by filling them with hot tap water and placing them near your cooking area. Prepare your rings and new lids by placing them in pairs (one new lid nested with one clean ring) nearby. Assemble the funnel and ladle, as well, and place a kitchen towel on the countertop next to the pressure canner.

3. Turn on the burner, the one on which the canner is sitting, to warm. Pour out the hot water from one jar. Ladle hot soup into the jar, leaving 1 inch of headspace. Apply new lids and rings fingertip tight to the jar and place it on the rack at the bottom of the pressure canner. Repeat the same procedure for each jar. Then, place the pressure canner lid on and secure according to the manufacturer's directions. Increase the heat to medium, and exhaust per the manufacturer's directions (typically for 10 minutes). Process at 11 pounds of pressure for 60 minutes for pint jars. When the time is up, turn the burner off and do *nothing* until the pressure valve on your pressure canner lid is completely released/flush with the lid and the dial indicates 0 pounds of pressure.

Basic (but Not Boring) Vegetables

In water-bath canning, vegetables are only possible when pickled. The acid in the vinegar makes them shelf-stable when coupled with the boiling water bath. Because we're pressure canning, however, we can preserve basic (but not boring) vegetables without the addition of an acidifying ingredient. I'll include recipes for vegetables that I believe give the best result and are the most useful when pressure canned. (You won't find any mushy canned spinach in this section!)

BEETS

YIELD: 7 QUARTS

Canning beets is best done with small beets 1 to 2 inches in diameter. Beets larger than this can be tough and stringy. Larger beets can be preserved but must be cut into chunks of about 1 to 2 inches in size. A whole beet can be a very pretty preserve, so I recommend smaller beets for that reason. However, you can cut larger beets into chunks or slice them into flat rounds.

YOU WILL NEED

21 pounds whole beets (yes, they're heavy!), tops removed

1. Scrub beets and cut off the green tops. Also, leave an inch of stem at the roots to prevent the beautiful red color from bleeding. Leave small beets whole; cut larger beets into chunks or slice into rounds that will fit into your jars. Cover beets with water and boil for 20 minutes. Remove beets to cool. When cool enough to handle, remove skins.

2. Boil a kettle of water.

3. Prepare your pressure canner. Fill the pot with hot water in the amount specified by the manufacturer (2 to 3 quarts is typical). Warm your jars by filling them with hot tap water and placing them near your cooking area. Prepare your rings and new lids by placing them in pairs (one new lid nested with one clean ring) nearby. Assemble the funnel and ladle, as well, and place a kitchen towel on the countertop next to the pressure canner.

4. Turn on the burner, the one on which the canner is sitting, to warm. Pour out the hot water from one jar. Ladle hot beets into the jar and pour hot water from the kettle on top of the beets, leaving 1 inch of headspace. Apply new lids and rings fingertip tight to the jar and place it on the rack at the bottom of the pressure canner. Repeat the same procedure for each jar. Then, place the pressure canner lid on and secure according to the manufacturer's directions. Increase the heat to medium, and exhaust per the manufacturer's directions (typically for 10 minutes). Process at 11 pounds of pressure for 30 minutes for pint jars and 35 minutes for quart jars. When the time is up, turn the burner off and do *nothing* until the pressure valve on your pressure canner lid is completely released/flush with the lid and the dial indicates 0 pounds of pressure.

GREEN OR WAX BEANS

YIELD: 7 QUARTS

The smell of freshly picked green beans is one I remember very fondly from childhood. My mom would give our garden-fresh green beans to us kids and tell us to snap the stems off before she cooked them for supper. Preserve your own with this simple recipe and enjoy farmers' market flavor in the dead of winter. You can choose to preserve them in 1-inch pieces, and if so, don't be shy in soliciting help from your pals or kids.

YOU WILL NEED

14 pounds green or wax beans (note: preserve the best beans you can and do not preserve soft, damaged beans or beans that aren't crisp and brightly colored)

1 teaspoon salt per quart, if desired

1. Wash and trim ends of beans. Leave as "whole" or snap into 1-inch sections if desired.

2. Boil a kettle of water.

3. Prepare your pressure canner. Fill the pot with hot water in the amount specified by the manufacturer (2 to 3 quarts is typical). Warm your jars by filling them with hot tap water and placing them near your cooking area. Prepare your rings and new lids by placing them in pairs (one new lid nested with one clean ring) nearby. Assemble the funnel and ladle, as well, and place a kitchen towel on the countertop next to the pressure canner.

4. Fill jars with raw beans as snuggly as you can and cover with hot water from the kettle, leaving 1 of inch headspace. Add 1 teaspoon salt per quart, if desired. Apply new lids and rings fingertip tight to the jar and place it on the rack at the bottom of the pressure canner. Repeat the same procedure for each jar. Then, place the pressure canner lid on and secure according to the manufacturer's directions. Increase the heat to medium, and exhaust per the manufacturer's directions (typically for 10 minutes). Process at 11 pounds of pressure for 20 minutes for pint jars and 25 minutes for quart jars. When the time is up, turn the burner off and do *nothing* until the pressure valve on your pressure canner lid is completely released/flush with the lid and the dial indicates 0 pounds of pressure.

CORN (WHOLE KERNEL)

YIELD: 7 QUARTS

Corn and other vegetables canned plain using a pressure canner are an enduring symbol of a home garden's bounty. They are the trophies from months of watering and weeding, pest deterring, and careful garden management. Whether you grow your own corn for this recipe or source it elsewhere, you'll love pulling these jars from your pantry. Note: Before selecting your jar size, take a look at the processing times. The processing time for pints of whole kernel corn is 55 minutes, and for quarts is 85 minutes. Not only is that a huge increase in time from pint to quart, it's also longer than many other vegetables. Plan accordingly.

YOU WILL NEED

32 pounds sweet corn* in
   their husks

1. Remove the corn husks and silks, then wash the cobs. While husking, boil a large pot of water for blanching the cobs. Submerge each cob *carefully* in boiling water to blanch for about a minute. Remove the blanched cobs. When cool enough to handle, slice the kernels off the cobs, slicing only the first ¾ of each kernel and leaving ¼ of each kernel on the cobs. *Be sure not to scrape the cobs.* Feed cobs to livestock or compost.

2. For each quart of kernels, add 1 cup hot water to a heavy bottomed pot. Bring the water and corn kernels to a boil and simmer for about 5 minutes.

3. Prepare your pressure canner. Fill the pot with hot water in the amount specified by the manufacturer (2 to 3 quarts is typical). Warm your jars by filling them with hot tap water and placing them near your cooking area. Prepare your rings and new lids by placing them in pairs (one new lid nested with one clean ring) nearby. Assemble the funnel and ladle, as well, and place a kitchen towel on the countertop next to the pressure canner.

4. Turn on the burner, the one on which the canner is sitting, to warm. Pour out the hot water from one jar. Ladle hot corn and water mixture into the jar, leaving 1 inch of headspace. Take care not to press or compact the corn. Apply new lids and rings fingertip tight to the jar and place it on the rack at the bottom of the pressure canner. Repeat

*Choose corn that's a little underripe or just ripe for eating fresh. Pressure canning will not improve the quality of older corn and in fact it will be quite tough.

the same procedure for each jar. Then, place the pressure canner lid on and secure according to the manufacturer's directions. Increase the heat to medium, and exhaust per the manufacturer's directions (typically for 10 minutes). Process at 11 pounds of pressure for 55 minutes for pint jars and 85 minutes for quart jars. When the time is up, turn the burner off and do *nothing* until the pressure valve on your pressure canner lid is completely released/flush with the lid and the dial indicates 0 pounds of pressure.

WHITE POTATOES

YIELD: 9 PINTS OR 7 QUARTS

By following this simple recipe, you can stock your shelves with the best quality spuds and really speed up a future meal's prep time! Be sure to take the time to peel the potatoes thoroughly, as safe canning practice calls for the removal of botulinum-bearing skins. Note: You have the option of canning whole or diced potatoes. If you choose whole, be aware you'll be precooking them for a longer amount of time, and you'll need to choose potatoes that are no more than 2 inches in diameter.

YOU WILL NEED

20 pounds potatoes

½ teaspoon salt per pint jar or 1 teaspoon salt per quart jar

Optional: ascorbic acid solution (see box directly below this recipe)

1. Wash and thoroughly peel potatoes. I recommend placing each potato in an ascorbic acid solution after peeling. Dice each potato into ½-inch pieces.

2. Bring a pot of water to boil. Boil potato pieces for 2 minutes. Whole potatoes need to be boiled for 10 minutes. Drain.

3. Prepare your pressure canner. Fill the pot with hot water in the amount specified by the manufacturer (2 to 3 quarts is typical). Warm your jars by filling them with hot tap water and placing them near your cooking area. Prepare your rings and new lids by placing them in pairs (one new lid nested with one clean ring) nearby. Assemble the funnel and ladle, as well, and place a kitchen towel on the countertop next to the pressure canner.

4. Turn on the burner, the one on which the canner is sitting, to warm. Pour out the hot water from one jar. Fill jars with hot potatoes and fresh, hot water, leaving 1 inch of headspace. Add ½ teaspoon salt to each pint jar or 1 teaspoon salt to each quart jar. Apply new lids and rings fingertip tight to the jar and place it on the rack at the bottom of the pressure canner. Repeat the same procedure for each jar. Then, place the pressure canner lid on and secure according to the manufacturer's directions. Increase the heat to medium, and exhaust per the manufacturer's directions (typically for 10 minutes). Process at 11 pounds of pressure for 35 minutes for pint jars and 40 minutes for quart jars. When the time is up, turn the burner off and do *nothing* until the pressure valve on your pressure canner lid is completely released/flush with the lid and the dial indicates 0 pounds of pressure.

ASCORBIC ACID SOLUTION TO PREVENT DARKENING

Not only is vitamin C the world's go-to for immunity boosting power, but it also prevents fruit and vegetables from darkening when exposed to air. There are several ways to treat foods with ascorbic acid before canning to prevent darkening or browning. You can use commercially prepared, store-bought ascorbic acid combined with citric acid. These mixes are desirable, because they're readily available; however, they're not quite as effective as plain ascorbic acid. You can instead buy plain 500 milligram vitamin C tablets, which are available at most grocery stores. Crush six 500 milligram tablets (totaling 3,000 milligrams) per gallon of water to treat your produce (via soaking or dunking). Another option is pure powdered ascorbic acid, which can be found in some stores, usually sold in the canning section. Follow the directions on the package to add this powder to water to create a solution. The extra step of pretreating your produce is worth it, I think, to preserve foods that will eventually look appetizing and won't make you (or the recipient of your canned gifts) second guess your canning practice. Foods that look browned will make you or gift recipients wonder if something went wrong in the canning process. Fortunately, the use of good old vitamin C will bring clarity to your canning.

ROASTED PEPPERS

YIELD: 8 PINTS (1 POUND PEPPERS = ABOUT 1 PINT PRESSURE CANNED PEPPERS)

Peppers are one of my favorite vegetables to can for a few reasons. They're so versatile and can completely replace a variety of store-bought peppers . . . and in fact these roasted peppers often end up being far superior. They take hot meat-and-cheese sandwiches from ho-hum to humdinger easily. The pressure canning process also tempers the spice, so instead of just feeling fire in your mouth, you can really taste the flavor of the peppers! Note: This recipe is undeniably more time-intensive because it takes time to peel the peppers. I almost always can this recipe over two days: one day for roasting and peeling, and the next day for pressure canning.

YOU WILL NEED

8 pounds sweet, mild, or hot peppers (most pressure canners hold 8–9 pints, unstacked, so I suggest getting a canning friend or family member to help you, and canning 8 pounds of peppers)

½ teaspoon salt per pint jar

1. Choose firm peppers for best results. You can also choose to preserve this recipe in half pints, which mimic more closely the small can sizes you might get at the grocery store of similar (but of course subpar) roasted peppers. If you plan to use hot peppers, use gloves to protect your skin, and do not touch your face. Wash your hands thoroughly after handling hot peppers. My recommendation is for peppers to be left whole, as I find it easiest to turn whole peppers under heat (which you'll be doing next), but they can be halved.

2. First, blister the skins. This can be done in a variety of ways, but you essentially need to use heat to blister the skin of the peppers. Using the oven to blister the skins, place the peppers directly on the rack of an oven set to 400°F. Turn over with tongs carefully after 4 or 5 minutes for a total of 8 to 10 minutes in the oven. This method is my preferred option. Using the stovetop (either gas or electric) to blister the skins, use metal tongs to place peppers one at a time over the direct heat of the burner, blistering each pepper, rotating slowly over high heat. Remove each blistered pepper from the heat, place in a bowl, and cover with a lid or cloth. Let the peppers cool and sweat.

3. Once blistered and cooled, prepare to peel by washing the peppers. The skins can be peeled by hand or with the help of a knife. Remove the cores and seeds. (This is no doubt a time-consuming process best helped by a friend with whom you need to catch up, with a cold drink tableside!)

4. Peppers can then be diced or sliced into sizes that would be most useful to you. I like them diced, but have also canned them in huge slices, fit for a chili burger.

5. Boil a kettle of water.

6. Prepare your pressure canner. Fill with hot water in the amount specified by the manufacturer (2 to 3 quarts is typical). Warm your jars by filling them with hot tap water and placing them near your cooking area. Prepare your rings and new lids by placing them in pairs (one new lid nested with one clean ring) nearby. Assemble the funnel and ladle, as well, and place a kitchen towel on the countertop next to the pressure canner.

7. Turn on the burner, the one on which the canner is sitting, to warm. Pour out the hot water from one jar. Pack peppers into the hot jar, leaving 1 inch of headspace. Pour boiling water from the kettle over the peppers (that is, pour the hot water to fill in the gaps between the peppers) and add ½ teaspoon salt, maintaining 1 inch of headspace. Apply new lids and rings fingertip tight to the jar and place it on the rack at the bottom of the pressure canner. Repeat the same procedure for each jar. Then, place the pressure canner lid on and secure according to the manufacturer's directions. Increase the heat to medium, and exhaust per the manufacturer's directions (typically for 10 minutes). Process at 11 pounds of pressure for 35 minutes for pint jars. When the time is up, turn the burner off and do *nothing* until the pressure valve on your pressure canner lid is completely released/flush with the lid and the dial indicates 0 pounds of pressure.

TOMATO JUICE

YIELD: 7 QUARTS

Tomatoes are rich in vitamins B, C, and potassium. You can use this recipe to make your own superior rendition of the store-bought tomato juice, also knowing it's a healthy way to start your morning (instead of a sugar rush from a glass of commercially made fruit juice). Important note #1: When canning tomato products, one issue that plagues canners is the separation of the red tomato goodness and the water content in the tomatoes. Read the directions below for tips on how to avoid this separation, but know that separation is normal and not unsafe in any way. It simply isn't as visually appealing. If your tomato juice separates, don't despair: simply shake before opening your jar. Important note #2: This recipe calls for the use of a food mill. If you don't have one, you can use a blender, but you'll just have a thicker juice, which is fine.

YOU WILL NEED

23 pounds tomatoes,
 washed and cored
½ teaspoon citric acid per
 quart jar

1. Have a heavy bottomed stockpot on the burner, ready to be filled with tomatoes. To avoid separated tomato juice, cut 1 pound (2–3) tomatoes into quarters and add them directly to the pot, turning the burner to high as you do so, then immediately bring to a boil while crushing them. (I use a wooden spoon, but you can use a large metal spoon or potato masher, as well.) Once boiling, add freshly quartered tomatoes, one at a time, to the boiling mixture. Quarter, add, crush, repeat. Keep the tomatoes boiling vigorously as you work. Once the last tomato is added, boil for 5 more minutes. If you don't worry about things like separated juice, simply quarter your tomatoes and heat and crush while the heat is on medium high, then bring to a boil for about 10 minutes once all are crushed and in the pot.

2. Ladle juice and pulp mixture from either process into the hopper of a food mill set atop another cooking pot or bowl and press through. If you don't have access to a food mill, use a blender to blitz smooth. Heat tomato juice to near boiling if it cooled significantly during the milling or blending process.

3. Prepare your pressure canner. Fill the pot with hot water in the amount specified by the manufacturer (2 to 3 quarts is typical). Warm your jars by filling them with hot tap water and placing them near your cooking area. Prepare your rings and new lids by placing them in pairs (one new lid nested with one clean ring) nearby. Assemble the funnel and ladle, as well, and place a kitchen towel on the countertop next to the pressure canner.

4. Turn on the burner, the one on which the canner is sitting, to warm. Pour out the hot water from one jar. Ladle hot tomato juice into the jar, leaving 1 inch of headspace. Apply new lids and rings fingertip tight to the jar and place it on the rack at the bottom of the pressure canner. Repeat the same procedure for each jar. Then, place the pressure canner lid on and secure according to the manufacturer's directions. Increase the heat to medium, and exhaust per the manufacturer's directions (typically for 10 minutes). Process at 11 pounds of pressure for 20 minutes for quart jars. When the time is up, turn the burner off and do *nothing* until the pressure valve on your pressure canner lid is completely released/flush with the lid and the dial indicates 0 pounds of pressure.

FOOD MILLS

In an age of advanced kitchen technology, where a home chef can look forward to the next novel device designed to make cooking easier, faster, and thus, better, I must take this opportunity to opine my love for the humble, analog food mill. A food mill has a hopper in which you put your food, cooked or uncooked. You turn the hand crank, and the grinding plate presses the food against sieve holes, pressing the smoothly pureed goodness through, leaving the seeds, skins, cores, and rough bits behind. It's ingenious, irreplaceable, and oh so valuable in canning and general cooking. The proverbial work horse, a food mill will never stop working, even if it has sat idle for years in your cupboard. No circuit will short, as it has none. It is low-tech perfection. On a personal note, I was given mine at a baby shower and use it all the time. This tomato juice recipe is the perfect example of when to bring out the food mill. Just quarter the tomatoes, heat them a bit to release the skins, ladle them into the food mill set atop a bowl, spin the handle, and ta-da, the skins remain above, and the pureed tomato goodness falls below. Most food mills come with different plates you can easily swap out, so you can use fine-holed plates for supersmooth puree and larger-holed plates for chunkier puree. Trust me, having one of these amazing tools in your kitchen when pressure canning may end up turning a previously laborious task into more of a rhythmic Zen movement. All hail the modest but mighty food mill!

(Continued on next page)

A FEW FACTS ABOUT TOMATOES

In the canning ethos, tomatoes are an intriguing vegetable, indeed. They're assumed by most people to be very high in acid, I believe, because we eat foods with tomatoes in them that tend to cause indigestion (think late-night pizza slices). Tomatoes are, in fact, very close to the not-quite-acidic-enough pH value of 4.6 required for water-bath canning, and if not acidified, must be pressure canned. This means tomatoes are less acidic than strawberries, apples, raspberries, lemons, and much more. Tomatoes, no matter if you grew them yourself with seeds you saved from your grandmother's garden or from commercially sourced seeds, will all be very close to the critical 4.6 mark on the pH scale.

Tomatoes have been bred over and over for ages to be redder, sweeter, and thus more alkaline. If your granny canned tomatoes (likely with no acidifying ingredient), it's very possible her tomatoes were much more acidic than those grown today. This observation brings us to the current state of tomatoes and canning today. With an acidifying ingredient such as citric acid, vinegar, or store-bought lemon juice (that is, a standardized acid level of 5 percent), tomato products can be safely preserved in a water-bath canning process. They can *also* be preserved in a pressure canner.

In a water-bath process, many tomato product processing times can be as long as forty minutes or more, so it becomes close to a tie, timewise, to pressure can the same recipe. For example, to pressure can a pint of tomato juice, you must process it for twenty minutes. The same tomato juice needs to be processed in a water-bath canner for thirty-five minutes, but the pressure canner must have been exhausted for ten minutes prior to processing. The decision to water-bath or pressure can tomatoes comes down to either personal preference, *or* if your tomato recipe has too many other low-acid ingredients that drive it into low-acid territory, it should be preserved via a pressure canning process. Also interesting is the fact that green or underripe tomatoes are more acidic than their rosy-ripe counterparts, so they may be safely canned using these recipes in a pressure canner. Warning: You should not can, using *either* process, tomatoes of any color coming from dead or frost-killed plants.

CRUSHED TOMATOES

YIELD: 7 QUARTS

A can of crushed tomatoes is one food item you may simply reach for at the grocery store, which you can soon replace with your own homemade jars. Just use this recipe! But be aware: It calls into question the decision to can plainly or season each jar. That is, you can either preserve these tomatoes plain, with just a bit of salt and the required citric acid, or you can choose to season your jars of crushed tomatoes with Italian-style herbs, garlic, or other seasonings, all of which can be delicious! I tend to season my jars more plainly so they can be seasoned on the fly, but I do see the wisdom in having at least a few jars boasting the spices of the Mediterranean or American Southwest, for example. It is ultimately up to you, and I encourage you to test out each methodology for yourself. Pressure canning allows for the flexibility of added garlic, spices, and all the extra flavor-oomph that water-bath canning can't, so consider a spoonful of minced chili or garlic per jar, if it strikes you.

YOU WILL NEED

22 pounds tomatoes, washed and cored

1 teaspoon salt per quart jar

½ teaspoon citric acid per quart jar

1. Boil a pot of water and prepare a separate ice bath in a bowl or the sink. Drop tomatoes a few at a time in the boiling water for about a minute. Remove using a slotted spoon and place in the ice bath. When cool enough to handle, slip off the skins.

2. Initially quarter about ¼ of the tomatoes; I find this part to be the messiest of all tomato processes, so one tool I appreciate is a cutting board with a trough to catch the copious tomato juices released in this process. Add the quartered tomatoes to a heavy bottomed pot, turn the heat up to high, and quickly bring them to a boil, crushing them with a wooden spoon, large metal spoon, or potato masher as they are heated. Be aware: You'll be working quickly to do this. Once the first quarter of the batch is crushed and boiling, quarter a few more at a time, adding to the pot, and returning to quartering. They don't need to be crushed, but you should stir them as you add them. Boil the tomatoes for 5 minutes once they are all in the pot together.

3. Prepare your pressure canner. Fill the pot with hot water in the amount specified by the manufacturer (2 to 3 quarts is typical). Warm your jars by filling them with hot tap water and placing them near your cooking area. Prepare your rings and new lids by placing them in pairs (one new lid nested with one clean ring) nearby. Assemble the funnel and ladle, as well, and place a kitchen towel on the countertop next to the pressure canner.

(Continued on page 65)

4. Turn on the burner, the one on which the canner is sitting, to warm. Pour out the hot water from one jar. Ladle hot tomatoes into the jar, leaving 1 inch of headspace. Add 1 teaspoon salt and ½ teaspoon citric acid to each quart jar. Apply new lids and rings fingertip tight to the jar and place it on the rack at the bottom of the pressure canner. Repeat the same procedure for each jar. Then, place the pressure canner lid on and secure according to the manufacturer's directions. Increase the heat to medium, and exhaust per the manufacturer's directions (typically for 10 minutes). Process at 11 pounds of pressure for 20 minutes for quart jars. When the time is up, turn the burner off and do *nothing* until the pressure valve on your pressure canner lid is completely released/flush with the lid and the dial indicates 0 pounds of pressure.

SAVE YOUR TOMATO SKINS

The skins saved from all this tomato peeling can be dehydrated in a 200°F oven or on the trays of a dehydrator set to 145°F. Season the velvety insides, if you can get to them, with powdered chili, garlic salt, tabasco, and/or other hot sauce and dry until crisp. Store in an airtight container. Crumble to use when you need a tomatoey burst of flavor when tomato season is long gone.

WHOLE CHERRY TOMATOES

YIELD: 9 PINTS

These tiny, sweet treats are useful far beyond a Bloody Mary garnish, of course, but they do make an ideal addition to the perfect brunch cocktail. Choose slightly underripe or at least firm cherry tomatoes for this recipe so they hold their shape. Notice these are not canned with any other liquid. *They'll be ruby red orbs ready for adding to your Perfectly Preserved Bloody Mary (page 67), beef stew, or pasta alfredo on the coldest night of the year . . . the choice is yours!* As a reminder, this recipe has a half-inch headspace requirement, which is different from most recipes in this book. *Maintain proper headspace as directed, and you'll have safely sealed jars in a very quick processing time (just 10 minutes in a pressure canner).*

YOU WILL NEED

13 pounds firm cherry tomatoes (any variety or color will do, though red will can well and yellow may darken to a browner hue), washed

½ teaspoon salt per pint jar

¼ teaspoon citric acid per pint jar

1. Boil a pot of water and prepare a separate ice bath in a bowl or the sink. Drop the cherry tomatoes in the boiling water for about a minute. Retrieve the tomatoes with a slotted spoon and place in the ice bath. When cool enough to handle, slip off the skins.

2. Prepare your pressure canner. Fill the pot with hot water in the amount specified by the manufacturer (2 to 3 quarts is typical). Warm your jars by filling them with hot tap water and placing them near your cooking area. Prepare your rings and new lids by placing them in pairs (one new lid nested with one clean ring) nearby. Assemble the funnel and ladle, as well, and place a kitchen towel on the countertop next to the pressure canner.

3. Turn on the burner, the one on which the canner is sitting, to warm. Pour out the hot water from one jar. Ladle in hot, whole tomatoes, ½ teaspoon salt, and ¼ teaspoon citric acid into the jar, leaving ½ inch of headspace. Apply new lids and rings fingertip tight to the jar and place it on the rack at the bottom of the pressure canner. Repeat the same procedure for each jar. Then, place the pressure canner lid on and secure according to the manufacturer's directions. Increase the heat to medium, and exhaust per the manufacturer's directions (typically for 10 minutes). Process at 11 pounds of pressure for 10 minutes for pint jars. When the time is up, turn the burner off and do *nothing* until the pressure valve on your pressure canner lid is completely released/flush with the lid and the dial indicates 0 pounds of pressure.

PERFECTLY PRESERVED BLOODY MARY

YIELD: 1 COCKTAIL

The Bloody Mary cocktail is a brunch classic but won't give you the same sugar rush as a mimosa. I like this drink on a hot day with an array of impressive skewers of pickled and fresh veggies, cheeses, sticks of bacon, peppers, and more. I've collected here some tasty options you can use to assemble this Perfectly Preserved Bloody Mary. Cheers!

YOU WILL NEED

Optional: lime wedge and coarse salt, to rim the glass

8 ounces Bloody Mary mix

2 ounces vodka (for a Bloody Maria, substitute tequila)

1 tablespoon Grated Horseradish (page 69)

Pearl Onions (page 71), to garnish

Asparagus Spears (page 73), to garnish

Mixed Vegetables (page 74), to garnish

1. If a salted rim is desired, rub the rim of a highball or pilsner glass with a lime wedge and dip the moistened edge into a saucer of coarse salt. This salt can be seasoned, as well; use your culinary creativity to season as you wish!

2. Fill glass with ice.

3. In a cocktail shaker filled with ice, combine the Bloody Mary mix, vodka or tequila, and Grated Horseradish. Shake well and pour into a prepared glass. Garnish with Pearl Onions, Asparagus Spears, Mixed Vegetables, and more!

CELERY STALK STIR STICKS

Unfortunately, celery doesn't can well. Choose fresh stalks that have abundant leafy greens on top for a fresh Bloody Mary garnish. More is more, in this case. Wash well and use the stalks as stir sticks.

BACON STIR STICKS

You may not know how to get stiff sticks of bacon—for stirring your Perfectly Preserved Bloody Mary—so here's an approach you can use! Once I learned this trick for cooking bacon in the oven, I never looked back. (And by the way, it's a far better method of "makin' bacon," no matter your desired stiffness.) Use thick cut, peppered, best quality bacon. Place slices on a sheet pan, not touching each other, then set in a 375°F oven for twenty-five minutes, checking at fifteen minutes and rotating your pan to cook the bacon evenly if your bacon is cooking unevenly (mine always is!). Cook till darkish red brown in color, then remove from the oven. Use a spatula to transfer the bacon to a cooling rack with paper towels beneath to let the fat drain off. The bacon will cool stiffly this way, but also will not be cooled in its own fat. Note: If you aren't sure whether the bacon is done, let one piece cool and if it isn't sufficiently stiff, cook the tray for an additional five minutes. Watch carefully, as you can go from done to overdone very quickly.

GRATED HORSERADISH

Although there are no safe, tested methods for pressure canning horseradish, I wanted to share a great little refrigerator pickle recipe here for your own grated horseradish. Add this to your freshly prepared Perfectly Preserved Bloody Mary (page 67) for some extra zing! A few notes: Horseradish root is best stored in a cool, dark place, as light is what turns the roots green, which is undesirable. Keep horseradish roots in a paper bag and store them in a cool place like the refrigerator until ready to use. The delicious pungency of horseradish fades quickly, so only make small quantities at a time. This isn't a recipe to double, unless you're sharing with friends.

YOU WILL NEED

2 pounds freshly washed
   and peeled horseradish
   root
1 cup best quality white
   vinegar, 5% acidity (not
   cider vinegar, as that will
   darken the horseradish)
½ teaspoon pickling or best
   quality additive-free salt
½ teaspoon ascorbic acid
   powder (see box on
   page 57)

1. Grate the horseradish with a box grater or food processor. Combine with remaining ingredients and fill into clean canning jars. Leave ¼ inch of headspace, add a clean lid and ring, and refrigerate. Use within 2 months.

PICKLING SALT

Pickling salt is salt with no additives. Additives prevent caking, among other things; but for canning purposes, additives will create a cloudy canning liquid (a.k.a. canning brine). While there's nothing inherently unsafe about using regular salt with additives, a cloudy brine isn't as visually appealing, and it also clouds your view of what's happening inside the jar. It's best to use pickling salt or another salt that's free of additives to give the best, clearest view into your jar and the quality therein. My recommendation? Use best quality additive-free salt whenever you can.

PEARL ONIONS

YIELD: 3 PINTS

These onions are as visually interesting as they are delicious! Pearl onions make a great addition to beef stews and can be pressure canned in small or large quantities. They're also a great item to use on charcuterie boards. Typically, there are few white preserved foods available for color-themed plates, but this is one of them!

YOU WILL NEED

2½ pounds red or white pearl onions (red onions turn a lovely pink when canned!)

½ cup plus 1 teaspoon salt, divided

1½ cups best quality white wine vinegar

1 teaspoon mustard seeds

1. Boil a pot of water. Submerge the onions in the boiling water for 1 to 2 minutes. Remove using a slotted spoon or pour into a colander. Transfer to an ice bath to cool. Prepare a separate cold water bath of 4 cups water and ½ cup salt. Slice off the ¼-inch root end of each onion and squeeze the onion out of its skin. This technique should work really well to peel these little onions for you. Place the peeled onions in the salt bath for 2 hours.

2. In a saucepan combine the remaining salt, white wine vinegar, and mustard seeds with the drained onions. Bring to a boil.

3. Prepare your pressure canner. Fill the pot with hot water in the amount specified by the manufacturer (2 to 3 quarts is typical). Warm your jars by filling them with hot tap water and placing them near your cooking area. Prepare your rings and new lids by placing them in pairs (one new lid nested with one clean ring) nearby. Assemble the funnel and ladle, as well, and place a kitchen towel on the countertop next to the pressure canner.

4. Fill jars with preserves (both onions and brine) leaving 1 inch of headspace. Apply new lids and rings fingertip tight, and place on the pressure canner rack. Secure the pressure canner lid. Exhaust as per the manufacturer's directions (typically for 10 minutes) and process for 40 minutes for both pints and quarts. When the time is up, turn the burner off and do nothing until the pressure valve on your pressure canner lid is completely released/flush with the lid and the dial indicates 0 pounds of pressure.

ASPARAGUS SPEARS

YIELD: 8 POUNDS = 3 PINT-AND-A-HALF JARS; 24 POUNDS YIELDS = 7 QUART JARS

Normally, I'd never pressure can something for a single recipe, nor for a single type of jar, but pickled asparagus spears beg to be canned for Bloody Marys! There are not a huge number of green vegetables that can be pressure canned without turning into mush, but asparagus cans well. These green veggies can be preserved in long spears in pint-and-a-half jars, if your pressure canner is tall enough (which preserves their shape nicely). Sidenote: A total of 6 pint-and-a-half jars fit in the Presto 16-quart pressure canner.

YOU WILL NEED

8 pounds tight-tipped
  asparagus spears, washed
  and trimmed of tough
  scales or bases
½ teaspoon salt per
  pint-and-a-half jar or
  1 teaspoon salt per
  quart jar

1. Boil a kettle of water.

2. Trim asparagus to spear size that will fit in pint-and-a-half jars.

3. Prepare your pressure canner. Fill the pot with hot water in the amount specified by the manufacturer (2 to 3 quarts is typical). Warm your jars by filling them with hot tap water and placing them near your cooking area. Prepare your rings and new lids by placing them in pairs (one new lid nested with one clean ring) nearby. Assemble the funnel and ladle, as well, and place a kitchen towel on the countertop next to the pressure canner.

4. Turn on the burner, the one on which the canner is sitting, to warm. Pour out the hot water from one jar. Pack the jar with raw, trimmed asparagus and ½ teaspoon salt per pint-and-a-half jar or 1 teaspoon per quart jar. Cover with hot water from the kettle, leaving 1 inch of headspace. Apply new lids and rings fingertip tight to the jar and place it on the rack at the bottom of the pressure canner. Repeat the same procedure for each jar. Then, place the pressure canner lid on and secure according to the manufacturer's directions. Increase the heat to medium, and exhaust per the manufacturer's directions (typically for 10 minutes). Process at 11 pounds of pressure for 40 minutes for either pint-and-a-half jars or quart jars. When the time is up, turn the burner off and do *nothing* until the pressure valve on your pressure canner lid is completely released/flush with the lid and the dial indicates 0 pounds of pressure.

MIXED VEGETABLES

YIELD: 6 QUARTS

Quarts of these mixed veggies can be added to soups or stews or served as a side dish quickly. Choose best quality vegetables seasonally and "shop" your pantry in the winter for these pressure canned wholesome basics!

YOU WILL NEED

6 cups fresh sweet corn (whole kernel)

6 cups fresh tomatoes

6 cups carrots

Optional: 2 tablespoons minced garlic

1 teaspoon salt per quart jar

1. Blanch peeled cobs of corn in boiling water for 3 minutes. Remove from boiling water bath and when cool enough to handle, slice the kernels off the cobs, slicing only the first ¾ of each kernel and leaving ¼ of each kernel on the cobs. *Be sure not to scrape the cobs.* Feed cobs to livestock or compost.

2. Core your washed tomatoes and blanch in a pot of boiling water for 1 minute. Remove the tomatoes with a slotted spoon and place them in an ice bath. When cool enough to handle, peel the tomatoes by hand. Roughly chop and add them to the heavy bottomed pot, including juices that may have accumulated.

3. Wash and peel the carrots. Slice into ¼ inch or smaller uniform pieces, then add to the pot.

4. Add enough water to cover, add garlic if desired, and bring to a boil. Boil for 5 minutes.

5. Prepare your pressure canner. Fill the pot with hot water in the amount specified by the manufacturer (2 to 3 quarts is typical). Warm your jars by filling them with hot tap water and placing them near your cooking area. Prepare your rings and new lids by placing them in pairs (one new lid nested with one clean ring) nearby. Assemble the funnel and ladle, as well, and place a kitchen towel on the countertop next to the pressure canner.

6. Turn on the burner, the one on which the canner is sitting, to warm. Pour out the hot water from one jar. Ladle the hot preserve and add 1 teaspoon salt into the jar, leaving 1 inch of headspace. Apply new lids and rings fingertip tight to the jar and place it on the rack at the bottom of the pressure canner. Repeat the same procedure for each jar. Then, place the pressure canner lid on and secure according to the manufacturer's directions. Increase the heat to medium, and

exhaust per the manufacturer's directions (typically for 10 minutes). Process at 11 pounds of pressure for 90 minutes for quart jars. When the time is up, turn the burner off and do *nothing* until the pressure valve on your pressure canner lid is completely released/flush with the lid and the dial indicates 0 pounds of pressure.

Hearty Jars

Meals in jars are the main reason people pressure can as a means of preservation. Broths and vegetables are great, but a jar that's a complete meal is really a revelation. The usefulness of home-canned chilis, stews, and soups can't be understated. While writing this book, I was amazed at how frequently I'd grab a half-pint jar (my test size) for lunch on the go. Once I'd have them on the shelf, I'd reach for them without hesitation. You may have thought, before reading this, you couldn't preserve meat and potatoes, for example, in the same jar; but you *can* and to great effect! This section will provide you with many examples of how to do so.

A number of these recipes ask you to brown your meat before canning. While this extra step may seem unnecessary, browning does two things for your meals in jars. It helps the meat keep its shape. I don't know about you, but I don't find mush appetizing. Browning in advance keeps your chunks of meat looking like meat and not like oatmeal. Precooking/browning *also* gives these dishes a similar taste to freshly cooked. I certainly didn't want any of these recipes to taste "canned" or tired, so I strived to have each taste like you cooked them today.

While I encourage you to precook when directions indicate, feel free to play with the spice level of all these recipes to suit your needs. You can add spice or heat into individual jars just before putting the lids on to create personalized jars for family members or friends. Just be sure to mark each lid with a permanent marker before placing it in the canner.

In this recipe section, you'll see a few bases for hearty soups. These bases are not canned with dairy, pasta, rice, or other grains, as those ingredients cannot be safely pressure canned. On each lid, after the base is canned and cooled, write a quick note about what to add to each jar. That way, when you're ready to warm up some Zuppa Toscana, you'll know to add the cream and kale upon reheating (for example). Another set of stars in this section is the various legumes I've selected for you to consider preserving. Definitely not sexy, but absolutely affordable and nutritious, and when pressure canned in these recipes, they're rock-star ingredients. "Beans, beans, the magical fruit . . ." are magical because they're full of fiber (which Americans, generally, can always use more of for health benefits), and are both filling and cost-effective for any thrifty homemaker. A reminder about beans: Get in the habit of soaking them overnight. Many times, I'll soak beans and not have a clear plan of what recipe I'll use the following day; but by having them ready, I've opened a wide set of possibilities for these little gems.

(Continued on next page)

These recipes take a bit more time, but the reward therein reflects that. Keep in mind you're cooking delicious, healthy meals in advance by pressure canning them. And the time you spend putting these soups and stews into jars will be saved (along with your sanity) later on, especially on busy weeknights. So, get ready to have your shelves full of hearty soups and stews, jars of homemade lunch for when you're busy or on the road, and giftable jars any new mother or friend in need would welcome.

Hearty Basics

Part of your pantry stocking process may include canning some hearty basics, and this next section will help you do just that. Jars of minimally seasoned meat will replace the "I forgot to defrost something for dinner!" panic with a sense of calm, as you open jars of shelf-stable, cooked meats. Free up freezer space, buy meat at a bargain, and can up these basics.

PRELIMINARY NOTES ABOUT PRESSURE CANNING GROUND MEAT

Specific guidance about pressure canning ground meat is given below (which includes some details about each type of meat discussed in this section), but one general bit regarding amounts that holds true for whatever meat you're using is 2 pounds of ground meat roughly yields 2 pints. Here are a few options to consider: ground beef, pork, sausage, veal, venison, and bear. I suggest you choose fresh, cold meat for all the following recipes. If you grind the meat yourself, keep in mind cold meat grinds much better than room temperature meat. Meat can be freshly defrosted or fresh (never frozen), but just make sure it's cold. All the following meats are safe for pressure canning and can be canned browned and unshaped, in patties, in meatballs (*without* egg or bread-crumbs), or in 3- to 4-inch links. Also, ground meat may be seasoned any way you like, but one teaspoon of salt per quart is a good starting amount. Brown the ground meat, fill the hot jars with the browned meat, and cover with Basic Bone Broth (page 35), Tomato Juice (page 60), which is especially good with wild game, or Plain Water (page 32), leaving 1 inch of headspace.

Ground beef

Ground beef is a staple of American kitchens and rightly so. It's so versatile and kid-friendly, not to mention easy to eat. Ground beef can be shaped into patties before browning, or balls, but don't be tempted to add egg or breadcrumbs to pressure canned meatballs, as those ingredients will prevent heat from penetrating effectively.

Ground pork

Ground pork can be pressure canned, giving you a handy base for many dishes, including those with a Western European flair, where pork is so popular. If you grind your own pork, take care to remove excess fat before grinding, as fat can inhibit a seal from forming during the canning process. Pressure canned ground pork can be especially helpful in enhancing a breakfast dish.

Ground sausage

Because sausage tends to be higher in fat, it's best for pressure canning if you choose the lowest-fat option available and drain as much fat as you can when browning/precooking. Sausage can be browned and canned without shaping (that is, canned "loose"), or can be canned in patties or links that are 3 to 4 inches long. Remember also that sage doesn't can well and can leave a bitter and unpleasant flavor. You can always add sage when you're reheating or as a garnish after opening the jar.

Ground venison

Naturally very lean, ground venison flavor is improved by incorporating one pound of pork fat with four pounds of venison at the grinding stage. Ask for this ratio from your butcher or do it yourself. I've used the meat grinder attachment for my KitchenAid mixer with great success, and this piece of kitchen equipment is at an affordable price point. It's safe to can venison without this fat addition, of course; but fat delivers excellent flavor and in this ratio you won't have to worry about the fat being in excess of what will stay safely in the jar, rather than climbing the sides and inhibiting a seal.

Ground bear

There are a few things to note when pressure canning this particular game meat. Ground bear is traditionally seasoned with sage, but should not be in this case, as sage gives a bitter, somewhat "off" flavor when canned. Bears that feed on fish or other ocean fare can have a fishy taste. Additionally, bears that feed on carrion can also have an unpleasant taste. Another consideration when preparing and eating bear is the nearly omnipresent trichinella (the same parasite that domestic hogs suffer from), but this parasite is killed at 160°F. The heat of the pressure canning process is more than sufficient to kill trichinella, so there's no need to be worried about it.

SOME FINAL NOTES ABOUT PRESSURE CANNED MEAT

At this point, there are two things needing your attention. Many times, your jars will be filled to the top, minus the one inch of headspace; and when they're done processing, you'll notice they'll only be half full. This is normal and safe. You'll get better with practice filling the jars, so they end up closer to three-quarters full; but I still sometimes get jars that shrink significantly. This is true of many pressure canned items, not just meat, but seems to happen to meat the most frequently and almost never to liquids.

Finally, canned meat sometimes ends up looking downright ugly. It can be so ugly that it was one of my chief concerns when writing this book; I worried how in the world I'd make canned meat look appetizing, while still in the jar. Do not let this deter you. The ugliness I'm referring to is that the meat can be sort of pale (especially if you raw pack) and any tough or fatty parts tend to press against the glass, like a sticky fingerprint smearing up your freshly washed windows. It can also end up being all slumped at the bottom, as if it's too tired to be served for a meal. Again, these issues are exacerbated if you raw pack instead of hot pack. Hot packed meat stands up much better, has better color, and is more appetizing in appearance. Still, I want to emphasize both ugly-looking meat and jars that were filled at the start and half-filled at the end are both acceptable *and* safe results of pressure canning.

GROUND MEAT

YIELD: 2 POUNDS GROUND MEAT = ROUGHLY 2 PINTS

YOU WILL NEED

2 pounds ground beef, pork, sausage, venison, or bear

2 tablespoons olive oil

½ teaspoon salt per pint jar or 1 teaspoon per quart jar

Plain Water (page 32), Basic Bone Broth (page 35), or store-bought* or home-canned Tomato Juice (page 60), to fill prepared jars

1. Brown the meat in the olive oil on all sides or roast in the oven. Half a teaspoon of salt per pint jar or 1 teaspoon per quart jar is a great starting point for seasoning, but you can season as heavily or as lightly as you wish. Add the browned meat to your jars and cover with the plain water, basic bone broth, or tomato juice.

2. Prepare your pressure canner. Fill the pot with hot water in the amount specified by the manufacturer (2 to 3 quarts is typical). Warm your jars by filling them with hot tap water and placing them near your cooking area. Prepare your rings and new lids by placing them in pairs (one new lid nested with one clean ring) nearby. Assemble the funnel and ladle, as well, and place a kitchen towel on the countertop next to the pressure canner.

3. Turn on the burner, the one on which the canner is sitting, to warm. Pour out the hot water from one jar. Ladle hot browned ground meat into the jar. Cover with plain water, basic bone broth, or tomato juice, leaving 1 inch of headspace. Apply new lids and rings fingertip tight to the jar and place it on the rack at the bottom of the pressure canner. Repeat the same procedure for each jar. Then, place the pressure canner lid on and secure according to the manufacturer's directions. Increase the heat to medium, and exhaust per the manufacturer's directions (typically for 10 minutes). Process at 11 pounds of pressure for 75 minutes for pint jars and 90 minutes for quart jars. When the time is up, turn the burner off and do *nothing* until the pressure valve on your pressure canner lid is completely released/flush with the lid and the dial indicates 0 pounds of pressure.

---

* Store-bought juices are sometimes required in canning recipes because they have a standardized acid value. I mention this because a canner may question if the addition of the tomato juice requires a standardized (that is, store-bought) acid value. This recipe is *not* dependent on the tomato juice to create a specific acid value, which is why home-canned is acceptable.

CUBED MEAT

YIELD: 2 POUNDS CUBED MEAT = ROUGHLY 3 PINTS

Pressure canning cubed meat is one of the most versatile and basic canning projects you can undertake. The pressure canning process makes meat remarkably tender, and browning the meat before canning helps the meat keep its shape and provides a superior flavor. It's safe to raw pack (pressure can without precooking or prebrowning), but I find hot packed (precooked or prebrowned) meat is more tender, not as mushy, and tastes much more like a freshly prepared meal. Raw packed pressure canned meat always seems like it needs to be cooked. It isn't raw, of course, because the heat of the pressure canning process cooks it sufficiently, but it lacks that "cooked" or browned taste we're so accustomed to. You can pressure can cubes of beef, pork, veal, lamb, venison, and bear using the following directions. Remember to remove excess fat, as fat is the enemy of a satisfactory seal. By the way, this method is one I use for the small pieces of venison that may otherwise be destined for jerky. It may be an unpopular opinion I hold, but I don't love making or eating jerky, as it's fairly labor-intensive and hard on my teeth to eat. Regardless, I feel the little bits of meat saved from the butchering process are wonderful when browned, seasoned, and canned. (They're also much easier on the teeth than jerky, shelf-stable far longer, and more versatile a food, as they can be added to tacos, served on rice or with potatoes, or eaten cold in a lunch box . . . my kids' favorite!)

YOU WILL NEED

2 pounds beef, pork, sausage, venison, or bear, cubed

2 tablespoons olive oil

½ teaspoon salt per pint jar or 1 teaspoon per quart jar

1. Brown the meat in the olive oil on all sides or roast in the oven. Half a teaspoon of salt per pint jar or 1 teaspoon per quart jar is a great starting point for seasoning, but you can season as heavily or as lightly as you wish. Add the browned meat to your jars and cover with Plain Water (page 32), Basic Bone Broth (page 35), or Tomato Juice (page 60).

2. Prepare your pressure canner. Fill the pot with hot water in the amount specified by the manufacturer (2 to 3 quarts is typical). Warm your jars by filling them with hot tap water and placing them near your cooking area. Prepare your rings and new lids by placing them in pairs (one new lid nested with one clean ring) nearby. Assemble the funnel and ladle, as well, and place a kitchen towel on the countertop next to the pressure canner.

3. Turn on the burner, the one on which the canner is sitting, to warm. Pour out the hot water from one jar. Ladle hot browned ground meat into the jar. Cover with plain water, basic bone broth, or tomato juice, leaving 1 inch of headspace. Apply new lids and rings fingertip tight to the jar and place it on the rack at the bottom of the pressure

(Continued on next page)

canner. Repeat the same procedure for each jar. Then, place the pressure canner lid on and secure according to the manufacturer's directions. Increase the heat to medium, and exhaust per the manufacturer's directions (typically for 10 minutes). Process at 11 pounds of pressure for 75 minutes for pint jars and 90 minutes for quart jars. When the time is up, turn the burner off and do *nothing* until the pressure valve on your pressure canner lid is completely released/flush with the lid and the dial indicates 0 pounds of pressure.

NOTE: Game meat can be soaked for one hour before canning in a brine of one tablespoon salt per quart water to mitigate a strong, gamey taste (especially if you suspect it to be present).

HOT PACKED, PLAIN, BONELESS CHICKEN

YIELD: 1 POUND CHICKEN = ABOUT 1 PINT

As a cattle rancher's daughter, I was in college before I realized how common meals prepared with chicken were to the rest of the world. At my childhood home, chicken was reserved for special occasions only, and I certainly never ate it canned until I was an adult. Now, I raise my own hens for eggs, and canning rooster (which has the same preparation and processing times as female birds) is on my canning bucket list. For those who don't have a mean rooster to send to the pantry shelf, canning chicken purchased at a bargain price can be an incredibly useful pantry staple. My favorite way to eat it is in a "mom salad" (that is, a salad with a lot of different ingredients like veggies and quinoa and maybe a "fancy" dressing if I'm really on the ball) while on our family's bass boat on the lake. Chicken is an effective vehicle for countless other flavors, too. Pressure can some and you'll be amazed at how often you reach for it!

YOU WILL NEED

1 pound chicken

1 tablespoon oil per pound of chicken

½ teaspoon salt per pint jar or 1 teaspoon salt per quart jar

1. Cut chicken into 1-inch pieces and brown in the oil, season as you like, and cook only until the chicken is browned on all sides. *The chicken does not need to be and should not be cooked all the way through.*

2. Prepare your pressure canner. Fill the pot with hot water in the amount specified by the manufacturer (2 to 3 quarts is typical). Warm your jars by filling them with hot tap water and placing them near your cooking area. Prepare your rings and new lids by placing them in pairs (one new lid nested with one clean ring) nearby. Assemble the funnel and ladle, as well, and place a kitchen towel on the countertop next to the pressure canner.

3. Turn on the burner, the one on which the canner is sitting, to warm. Pour out the hot water from one jar. Ladle hot chicken into the jar, leaving 1 inch of headspace. Cover the pieces with Basic Bone Broth (page 35) or Plain Water (page 32). If you cooked the chicken unseasoned, add ½ teaspoon salt per pint jar or 1 teaspoon per quart jar. Apply new lids and rings fingertip tight to the jar and place it on the rack at the bottom of the pressure canner. Repeat the same procedure for each jar. Then, place the pressure canner lid on and secure according to the manufacturer's directions. Increase the heat to medium, and exhaust per

(Continued on next page)

the manufacturer's directions (typically for 10 minutes). Process at 11 pounds of pressure for 75 minutes for pints and 90 minutes for quarts. When the time is up, turn the burner off and do *nothing* until the pressure valve on your pressure canner lid is completely released/flush with the lid and the dial indicates 0 pounds of pressure.

RAW PACKED, PLAIN, BONELESS CHICKEN

YIELD: 1 POUND CHICKEN = ABOUT 1 PINT

For raw packed chicken, there are usually enough juices to cover the meat during the pressure canning process so no water, broth, or other liquids are added to this recipe.

YOU WILL NEED

Cold, raw chicken cut into 1-inch pieces
1 teaspoon salt per quart jar

1. Prepare your pressure canner. Fill the pot with hot water in the amount specified by the manufacturer (2 to 3 quarts is typical). Warm your jars by filling them with hot tap water and placing them near your cooking area. Prepare your rings and new lids by placing them in pairs (one new lid nested with one clean ring) nearby. Assemble the funnel and ladle, as well, and place a kitchen towel on the countertop next to the pressure canner.

2. Turn on the burner, the one on which the canner is sitting, to warm. Pour out the hot water from one jar. Fill the warm jar with the cold, raw chicken pieces. Add 1 teaspoon salt per quart jar. Leave 1¼ inch headspace (¼ inch more than normal). No liquid should be added to the jar. Apply new lids and rings fingertip tight to the jar and place it on the rack at the bottom of the pressure canner. Repeat the same procedure for each jar. Then, place the pressure canner lid on and secure according to the manufacturer's directions. Increase the heat to medium, and exhaust per the manufacturer's directions (typically for 10 minutes). Process at 11 pounds of pressure for 75 minutes for pints and 90 minutes for quarts. When the time is up, turn the burner off and do *nothing* until the pressure valve on your pressure canner lid is completely released/flush with the lid and the dial indicates 0 pounds of pressure.

(Continued on next page)

DUCK, GOOSE, TURKEY, AND OTHER GAME BIRDS

Prepare as recipes for hot- or raw-packed boneless chicken above for pressure canning other poultry and game fowl. Waterfowl can be soaked in a brine of 1 quart water and 1 tablespoon salt for 1 hour before canning to reduce the gamey taste. Make sure to soak and rinse the meat before cutting it into pieces. Important note: If you brine poultry and game fowl before canning, you do not need to add more salt to the jars.

POULTRY WITH BONES

I've never canned meat with bones, because there's not a lot of room in jars; I want my jars filled with what I can eat! However, I wanted to give processing times for canning with bones, should you have a glut of wings, for example, and want to can with the bone in. I'll ruin the surprise for you now: Processing times are a bit shorter for bone-in chicken than boneless chicken! Prepare exactly as recipes for hot- or raw-packed boneless chicken above. For both hot- and raw-packed chicken *with* bones, process at 11 pounds of pressure for 65 minutes for pints and 75 minutes for quarts.

RABBIT

As small-scale homesteading continues to grow in popularity, meat rabbits are seeing a resurgence in popularity, as well. You can pressure can rabbit meat exactly as you would chicken. Prepare exactly as recipes for hot- or raw-packed boneless chicken above, and that includes canning with the bone in.

Hearty Meals in Jars

The heartiest meals in jars are found in this section. You'll find soups with beans and meat, stews, bold flavors, and classic combinations in both traditional and fresh, unique styles. These jars can be opened, heated, and eaten on the go, as fast-food-made-slowly.

In all the years I've been canning, it's recipes like these that make pressure canning extra fun! While canning pantry staples is great, hearty meals in jars are what drew me to pressure canning in the first place . . . and I bet will be what keeps me here many years from now, too. I hope you'll find some extra joy in the "old favorites" and new go-tos in this section.

GRAM'S HAMBURGER SOUP

YIELD: 5–6 PINTS

My grandmother, the quintessential rancher's wife and home cook, made this old-fashioned hamburger soup for winter meals, especially when feeding a large crew who'd been working cattle in the cold. It's one of the recipes I'm sure I'll remember forever! And hey, this recipe is flexible: double or halve it, if you prefer; season it nice and spicy, if you like; add more or less tomato, depending on your tastes; but do consider serving it with some buttered bread to dip in the broth, just like Gram would!

YOU WILL NEED

2 pounds ground beef

2 tablespoons olive oil

1 onion, diced

2 medium yellow potatoes, peeled and cubed into 1-inch pieces

2 carrots, peeled and diced

2 tomatoes, cored and diced, or 1 (14.5-ounce) can diced tomatoes

2 teaspoons seasoned salt or more to taste

1 (6-ounce) can tomato paste

1 tablespoon dried Italian herb seasoning

12 cups water

1. Brown the ground beef, drain, and set aside.

2. Heat the oil in a large, heavy bottomed pot, then brown the onion. Add in all remaining ingredients (including the browned beef) and heat to a boil, simmering for five minutes.

3. Prepare your pressure canner. Fill the pot with hot water in the amount specified by the manufacturer (2 to 3 quarts is typical). Warm your jars by filling them with hot tap water and placing them near your cooking area. Prepare your rings and new lids by placing them in pairs (one new lid nested with one clean ring) nearby. Assemble the funnel and ladle, as well, and place a kitchen towel on the countertop next to the pressure canner.

4. Turn on the burner, the one on which the canner is sitting, to warm. Pour out the hot water from one jar. Ladle hot soup into jars, leaving 1 inch of headspace. Apply new lids and rings fingertip tight to the jar and place it on the rack at the bottom of the pressure canner. Repeat the same procedure for each jar. Then, place the pressure canner lid on and secure according to the manufacturer's directions. Increase the heat to medium, and exhaust per the manufacturer's directions (typically for 10 minutes). Process at 11 pounds of pressure for 75 minutes for pint jars. When the time is up, turn the burner off and do *nothing* until the pressure valve on your pressure canner lid is completely released/flush with the lid and the dial indicates 0 pounds of pressure.

GRAM'S TACO SOUP

YIELD: 5–6 PINTS

My grandmother's recipe box also *contained this Mexican-style recipe for soup made with ground beef. It's even better when served with tortilla chips, a dollop of sour cream, some fresh, diced avocado, and shredded cheese.*

YOU WILL NEED

2 pounds ground beef, browned and drained

2 tablespoons olive oil

1 onion, diced

2 cups chopped tomatoes or 1 pint Crushed Tomatoes (page 63)

¾ cup dry kidney beans, soaked overnight, or 1 (10.5-ounce) can kidney beans

12 cups water or more, to reach desired consistency

3 teaspoons ground cumin

2 tablespoons chili powder

2 teaspoons salt

1 teaspoon paprika

½ teaspoon dried oregano

½ teaspoon garlic powder

½ teaspoon onion powder

Pinch cayenne pepper

1. Brown ground beef, drain, and set aside.

2. Heat the oil in a large, heavy bottomed pot and brown the onion. Add in all remaining ingredients (including the browned beef) and simmer for five minutes.

3. Prepare your pressure canner. Fill the pot with hot water in the amount specified by the manufacturer (2 to 3 quarts is typical). Warm your jars by filling them with hot tap water and placing them near your cooking area. Prepare your rings and new lids by placing them in pairs (one new lid nested with one clean ring) nearby. Assemble the funnel and ladle, as well, and place a kitchen towel on the countertop next to the pressure canner.

4. Turn on the burner, the one on which the canner is sitting, to warm. Pour out the hot water from one jar. Ladle hot soup into jars, leaving 1 inch of headspace. Apply new lids and rings fingertip tight to the jar and place it on the rack at the bottom of the pressure canner. Repeat the same procedure for each jar. Then, place the pressure canner lid on and secure according to the manufacturer's directions. Increase the heat to medium, and exhaust per the manufacturer's directions (typically for 10 minutes). When the time is up, turn the burner off and do *nothing* until the pressure valve on your pressure canner lid is completely released/flush with the lid and the dial indicates 0 pounds of pressure.

CHILI CON CARNE

YIELD: 7 PINTS

One of my favorite aspects of pressure canning this recipe is you can add and adjust the seasonings to suit your preferences. You may alter and fine-tune the amount of onions, peppers, garlic, chilis, etc. to your heart's content, but keep the quantities close to the same as listed here. My experience has been the pressure canning process cooks the chili perfectly, and I hope you'll agree it's fabulous for a grab-and-go lunch!

YOU WILL NEED

4 cups water

2 cups dry kidney beans, soaked for 8 hours or overnight, drained

2 pounds ground beef

1 tablespoon garlic, finely chopped

1 cup onions, chopped

6 cups freshly chopped or canned tomatoes*

1 cup peppers of your choice (consider bell, yellow, or any of the hotter varieties, depending on your preference), chopped

Salt to taste

1. Add the 4 cups water and drained beans to a cooking pot and simmer on medium-low heat.

2. In a separate pan, brown the ground beef, garlic, and onions, and drain when the beef is browned. Do not overcook.

3. Add the ground beef mixture and the tomatoes and peppers to the beans. Cook till boiling, then turn heat to low, stirring occasionally.

4. Prepare your pressure canner. Fill the pot with hot water in the amount specified by the manufacturer (2 to 3 quarts is typical). Warm your jars by filling them with hot tap water and placing them near your cooking area. Prepare your rings and new lids by placing them in pairs (one new lid nested with one clean ring) nearby. Assemble the funnel and ladle, as well, and place a kitchen towel on the countertop next to the pressure canner.

5. Turn on the burner, the one on which the canner is sitting, to warm. Pour out the hot water from one jar. Ladle hot chili into the jar, leaving 1 inch of headspace. Apply new lids and rings fingertip tight to the jar and place it on the rack at the bottom of the pressure canner. Repeat the same procedure for each jar. Then, place the pressure canner lid on and secure according to the manufacturer's directions. Increase the heat to medium, and exhaust per the manufacturer's directions (typically for 10 minutes). Process at 11 pounds of pressure for 75 minutes for pint jars. When the time is up, turn the burner off and do *nothing* until the pressure valve on your pressure canner lid is completely released/flush with the lid and the dial indicates 0 pounds of pressure.

---

* If using freshly chopped tomatoes, drain the tomato juice. If using store-bought canned tomatoes, consider the Ro-Tel kind with peppers added, which I prefer. Or use fresh, as hot as you like them (roasted jalapeños are good).

ZUPPA TOSCANA BASE

YIELD: 5–6 PINTS

This recipe is a base, meaning you'll add heavy cream, kale, and a sprinkle of Parmesan cheese upon opening the jars. This is a great dupe of the Olive Garden restaurant staple, Zuppa Toscana. You could safely pressure can the kale, but pressure canning makes for very wilted greens, so I don't recommend it. I suggest adding kale after opening the jars to ensure they haven't been reduced to a dark green smudge.

YOU WILL NEED

2 tablespoons olive oil

½ onion, diced

1 tablespoon garlic, minced

1 pound mild or spicy ground Italian sausage, low-fat, if possible (remember, fat is the enemy of a reliable seal)

8 cups Basic Bone Broth (page 35), chicken stock, Vegetable Stock (page 41) and/or Plain Water (page 32); I often do half bone broth and half water to great results!

5 medium yellow potatoes, washed, peeled, and chopped into 1-inch pieces

2 tablespoons salt or to taste, depending on how salty your sausage is (start with 1 tablespoon and add more from there, and remember that salt gives the flavor that fat might have, if not in a canning jar)

¼ cup heavy cream per pint jar

½ cup kale per pint jar

Bacon bits and Parmesan cheese, to garnish

1. Heat the oil in a soup pot over medium-high heat and brown the onion and garlic until translucent and a bit browned.

2. In a separate stockpot, brown the sausage and drain all fat. Once the onions and garlic are browned, add the broth/stock and/or water, potatoes, and salt to the browned onion and garlic in the soup pot. Bring to a boil (you can cook this while you prepare the pressure canner).

3. Prepare your pressure canner. Fill the pot with hot water in the amount specified by the manufacturer (2 to 3 quarts is typical). Warm your jars by filling them with hot tap water and placing them near your cooking area. Prepare your rings and new lids by placing them in pairs (one new lid nested with one clean ring) nearby. Assemble the funnel and ladle, as well, and place a kitchen towel on the countertop next to the pressure canner.

4. Turn on the burner, the one on which the canner is sitting, to warm. Pour out the hot water from one jar. Ladle the hot preserve into the jar, leaving 1 inch of headspace. Apply new lids and rings fingertip tight to the jar and place it on the rack at the bottom of the pressure canner. Repeat the same procedure for each jar. Then, place the pressure canner lid on and secure according to the manufacturer's directions. Increase the heat to medium, and exhaust per the manufacturer's directions (typically for 10 minutes). Process at 11 pounds of pressure for 60 minutes for pint jars. When the time is up, turn the burner off and do *nothing* until the pressure valve on your pressure canner lid is completely released/flush with the lid and the dial indicates 0 pounds of pressure.

5. Upon reheating, add ¼ cup heavy cream and ½ cup kale per pint and heat through. Do not pressure can (or water-bath can, for that matter) any dairy products. Garnish this dish with bacon bits and Parmesan cheese, if desired.

MARINARA SAUCE

YIELD: ABOUT 7 QUARTS

A busy parent's ace in the hole, this all-in-one jar of wholesome, tasty tomato sauce with cooked ground meat is sure to be a true pantry superhero! If you need further convincing, look at the ingredient list of any store-bought marinara sauce. Not only are those jars expensive, but they're also usually full of added sugar and/or mystery ingredients you'd just rather not consume. Try this sauce, and season it however your (or someone else's!) Italian grandmother would, and you'll thank yourself later. You can double or triple this recipe but be sure to plan out how many batches you'll need to process.

YOU WILL NEED

15 pounds tomatoes

1 pound ground beef or sausage

2 tablespoons garlic, minced

½ cup onions, chopped

Optional: Additional ½ pound onions, sliced

2 teaspoons salt

1 tablespoon dried Italian herb seasoning or 2 drops best quality oregano oil and 2 drops best quality black pepper oil

1. Boil a large pot of water and drop in a few tomatoes at a time, letting them boil for 1 minute. Use a slotted spoon to retrieve the tomatoes and place them in an ice bath. When cool enough to handle, remove and discard the tomato skins, then core and quarter the tomatoes. Add the prepped tomatoes to a heavy bottomed pot and simmer for 15 minutes. Remove from heat and puree the tomatoes using an immersion blender, a standard blender, food processor or, my favorite analog tool for canning, a food mill. Alternatively, core and quarter the washed tomatoes first, then process in a blender until smooth. The point being, skins of washed tomatoes pose no safety concern in canning, and I don't have an Italian grandmother to dissuade me from doing so. Actually, I always use this method for tomato sauces, as it saves so much time and I never notice any tiny bits of tomato skin. Choose your method and prepare the tomatoes the day before canning if you prefer.

2. Brown the meat and drain the fat, then add the ground meat and all other ingredients (including your prepped tomatoes) to a heavy bottomed pot and bring to a boil. You can simmer this mixture for an hour or more to create a thicker sauce or leave it on the thinner side. Either way, stir often.

3. Prepare your pressure canner. Fill the pot with hot water in the amount specified by the manufacturer (2 to 3 quarts is typical). Warm your jars by filling them with hot tap water and placing them near your cooking area. Prepare your rings and new lids by placing them in pairs (one new lid nested

(Continued on next page)

with one clean ring) nearby. Assemble the funnel and ladle, as well, and place a kitchen towel on the countertop next to the pressure canner.

4. Turn on the burner, the one on which the canner is sitting, to warm. Pour out the hot water from one jar. Ladle hot sauce into the jar, leaving 1 inch of headspace. Apply new lids and rings fingertip tight to the jar and place it on the rack at the bottom of the pressure canner. Repeat the same procedure for each jar. Then, place the pressure canner lid on and secure according to the manufacturer's directions. Increase the heat to medium, and exhaust per the manufacturer's directions (typically for 10 minutes). Process at 11 pounds of pressure for 60 minutes for pint jars and 70 minutes for quart jars. When the time is up, turn the burner off and do *nothing* until the pressure valve on your pressure canner lid is completely released/flush with the lid and the dial indicates 0 pounds of pressure.

VINHA D'AHLOS PORTUGUESE PORK

YIELD: 6 PINTS

While this recipe is not a family recipe, my husband's Portuguese family had their own fermented version of vinha d'ahlos, which was prepared by his paternal grandmother. As is so common with the transfer of traditions and recipes from culture to culture and generation to generation, the name for this wine, vinegar, and pork recipe was said aloud to me as, "vinny-darlos." I never figured out what that recipe could be until I read the name for this classic Portuguese entrée when searching "Portuguese pork dishes" and realized they were one and the same. It features a strong wine and vinegar flavor and incredibly tender meat. This is one recipe I'll make year after year, in pints, to take for a delicious hot lunch on the go, as it's easily reheated in the jars I preserved it in.

YOU WILL NEED

¼ cup olive oil

3 pounds pork shoulder or butt, with fat trimmed, cut in 1-inch cubes

1 head garlic, peeled and diced fine

1 onion, diced in 1-inch chunks

1 celery stalk, diced in 1-inch pieces

2 carrots, peeled and diced in 1-inch pieces

4 russet potatoes, peeled and diced in 1-inch chunks

1½ cups white wine

2½ cups best quality apple cider vinegar

2 bay leaves

4 sprigs fresh thyme or 1 tablespoon dried thyme leaves

2 tablespoons soy sauce

1. Heat the oil in a heavy bottomed pot or skillet on high heat. Season the pork cubes with salt and pepper. Brown the pork pieces on each side and transfer to a plate when browned, taking care to drain the oil and fat after browning. In the same pot, brown all the veggies for up to five minutes, stirring. Add in the wine, vinegar, bay leaves, thyme, and soy sauce. Simmer with the lid on, stirring occasionally, for 1 hour. Remove the bay leaves and reduce the heat.

2. Prepare your pressure canner. Fill the pot with hot water in the amount specified by the manufacturer (2 to 3 quarts is typical). Warm your jars by filling them with hot tap water and placing them near your cooking area. Prepare your rings and new lids by placing them in pairs (one new lid nested with one clean ring) nearby. Assemble the funnel and ladle, as well, and place a kitchen towel on the countertop next to the pressure canner.

3. Turn on the burner, the one on which the canner is sitting, to warm. Pour out the hot water from one jar. Ladle the hot mixture into the jar, leaving 1 inch of headspace. Apply new lids and rings fingertip tight to the jar and place it on the rack at the bottom of the pressure canner. Repeat the same procedure for each jar. Then, place the pressure canner lid on and secure according to the manufacturer's directions. Increase the heat to medium, and exhaust per the manufacturer's directions (typically for 10 minutes). Process

(Continued on next page)

at 11 pounds of pressure for 75 minutes for pint jars and 90 minutes for quart jars. When the time is up, turn the burner off and do *nothing* until the pressure valve on your pressure canner lid is completely released/flush with the lid and the dial indicates 0 pounds of pressure.

SPLIT PEAS WITH PORK

YIELD: 5 PINTS

This is a hearty, super flavorful rendition of the classic split pea soup. Remember to remove as much fat as possible, as fat is the enemy of a good seal.

YOU WILL NEED

¼ pound pork shoulder or roast, cut into 1-inch cubes with as much fat removed as possible

2 cups dry split peas, soaked overnight

1 jalapeño pepper, deseeded and diced

1 teaspoon best quality salt or more to taste

4 cups Plain Water (page 32) or combination of water and Basic Bone Broth (page 35)

1. Brown the pork till crisp and browned on all sides.

2. Combine the browned pork with all other ingredients in a stockpot and bring to a boil.

3. Prepare your pressure canner. Fill the pot with hot water in the amount specified by the manufacturer (2 to 3 quarts is typical). Warm your jars by filling them with hot tap water and placing them near your cooking area. Prepare your rings and new lids by placing them in pairs (one new lid nested with one clean ring) nearby. Assemble the funnel and ladle, as well, and place a kitchen towel on the countertop next to the pressure canner.

4. Turn on the burner, the one on which the canner is sitting, to warm. Pour out the hot water from one jar. Ladle the hot preserve into the jar, leaving 1 inch of headspace. Apply new lids and rings fingertip tight to the jar and place it on the rack at the bottom of the pressure canner. Repeat the same procedure for each jar. Then, place the pressure canner lid on and secure according to the manufacturer's directions. Increase the heat to medium, and exhaust per the manufacturer's directions (typically for 10 minutes). Process at 11 pounds of pressure for 60 minutes for pint jars. When the time is up, turn the burner off and do *nothing* until the pressure valve on your pressure canner lid is completely released/flush with the lid and the dial indicates 0 pounds of pressure.

NAVY BEAN CHICKEN CHILI

YIELD: 4 PINTS

Wondering why these creamy beans aren't blue (as in the color navy blue)? Well, it turns out that in the early 1900s these beans were a staple for the US Navy. All beans are high in fiber, but this particular bean offers an impressive nineteen grams per cup. That means they're filling and nutritious, as well as inexpensive. Navy beans are also the creamiest of white beans, making this soup an ideal "comfort food" dish.

YOU WILL NEED

2 tablespoons olive oil

3 pounds chicken, cut into 1-inch pieces

1 onion, chopped

1 jalapeño pepper, deseeded and sliced

2 cups dry navy beans or other white beans like cannellini or white northern beans, soaked overnight

4 cups chicken broth, vegetable broth, or Plain Water (page 32)

1 cup or 1 (8-ounce) can roasted green peppers, diced

1 tablespoon cumin

1 teaspoon garlic salt

½ teaspoon chili powder

½ teaspoon black pepper

½ teaspoon paprika

1. In a deep pan, heat the oil on medium. Brown the chicken on all sides and remove from the pan. To the same pan, add the onion and jalapeño and cook until soft and translucent. Add the remaining ingredients and simmer for 30 minutes, or until beans are nearly tender.

2. Prepare your pressure canner. Fill the pot with hot water in the amount specified by the manufacturer (2 to 3 quarts is typical). Warm your jars by filling them with hot tap water and placing them near your cooking area. Prepare your rings and new lids by placing them in pairs (one new lid nested with one clean ring) nearby. Assemble the funnel and ladle, as well, and place a kitchen towel on the countertop next to the pressure canner.

3. Turn on the burner, the one on which the canner is sitting, to warm. Pour out the hot water from one jar. Ladle the hot preserve into the jar, leaving 1 inch of headspace. Apply new lids and rings fingertip tight to the jar and place it on the rack at the bottom of the pressure canner. Repeat the same procedure for each jar. Then, place the pressure canner lid on and secure according to the manufacturer's directions. Increase the heat to medium, and exhaust per the manufacturer's directions (typically for 10 minutes). Process at 11 pounds of pressure for 75 minutes for pint jars. When the time is up, turn the burner off and do *nothing* until the pressure valve on your pressure canner lid is completely released/flush with the lid and the dial indicates 0 pounds of pressure.

CHICKEN WITH POTATOES AND GARLIC

YIELD: 4–5 PINTS

This simple, but mighty appetizing recipe will shoulder the weight of a weekday supper readily and goes well with a fresh salad or roasted veggies. It's also quick to assemble and prepare.

YOU WILL NEED

2 tablespoons olive oil

2 tablespoons fresh garlic, minced, divided

4–5 cups chicken, beef, or other broth or Plain Water (page 32)

2 teaspoons salt

4 pounds chicken breast or tenders, cut into roughly 1-inch chunks

3 pounds yellow potatoes, peeled and cut into 1-inch chunks

1. Heat the oil in a heavy bottomed pan over medium heat. Add 1 tablespoon garlic and warm until fragrant. In a pot, set the broth or water to low so that it's warm and ready for you when the rest of the steps are completed. In another pan, salt and brown the chicken on all sides. Separately, steam or boil the potato chunks until about halfway cooked, about 15 minutes. Drain.

2. Prepare your pressure canner. Fill the pot with hot water in the amount specified by the manufacturer (2 to 3 quarts is typical). Warm your jars by filling them with hot tap water and placing them near your cooking area. Prepare your rings and new lids by placing them in pairs (one new lid nested with one clean ring) nearby. Assemble the funnel and ladle, as well, and place a kitchen towel on the countertop next to the pressure canner.

3. Turn on the burner, the one on which the canner is sitting, to warm. Pour out the hot water from the jars. Divide the remaining garlic and potatoes among the warm jars. Add the chicken, dividing evenly among the jars. Ladle the warm broth or water on top, leaving 1 inch of headspace.

4. Apply new lids and rings fingertip tight to the jar and place it on the rack at the bottom of the pressure canner. Repeat the same procedure for each jar. Then, place the pressure canner lid on and secure according to the manufacturer's directions. Increase the heat to medium, and exhaust per the manufacturer's directions (typically for 10 minutes). Process at 11 pounds of pressure for 75 minutes for pint jars and 90 minutes for quart jars. When the time is up, turn the burner off and do *nothing* until the pressure valve on your pressure canner lid is completely released/flush with the lid and the dial indicates 0 pounds of pressure.

CHICKEN CACCIATORE

YIELD: 6 PINTS

This hunter-style dish is homey, cozy, and oh-so-delicious! Your home will smell like fall as you cook, and the result will be tender bites of chicken, flavorful vegetables, and a filling meal . . . all in one jar.

YOU WILL NEED

3 tablespoons olive oil, divided

6 boneless, skinless chicken breasts, cut into 1-inch pieces

4 ounces small white mushrooms, sliced ¼-inch thick

1 small white onion, diced

2 small carrots, peeled and sliced into ¼-inch thick rounds

1 tablespoon fresh garlic, minced

¼ cup dry white wine

2 cups fresh or canned tomatoes, chopped, juices reserved

1 bell pepper, ribs, seeds, and stem removed, diced

½ cup Basic Bone Broth (page 32), Vegetable Stock (page 41), or Roasted Mushroom Stock (page 42)

6 sprigs rosemary (1 for each pint jar) or 1–2 drops rosemary oil

1. Heat 2 tablespoons oil in a large, heavy skillet over medium heat. Season the chicken with salt and pepper and brown the chicken on all sides. Transfer to a plate when the chicken is cooked halfway through or browned but still pink on the inside.

2. Wipe the skillet clean and heat the remaining oil on medium. Add the mushrooms and brown them, about 5 minutes. Transfer to the plate with the chicken. Turn the heat down to low, and add the onion, carrots, and garlic. Cook on low for about 10 minutes, stirring occasionally, until the onions are translucent. Add the wine and turn the heat to high, stirring constantly to remove the browned bits from the skillet, allowing the wine to cook off. This will take about 1 minute. Add the tomatoes, bell pepper, and broth or stock. Season with salt and pepper to taste, stirring to combine. Add in the browned chicken and mushrooms. Bring to a boil. Reduce the heat to low and simmer for 20 minutes.

3. Prepare your pressure canner. Fill the pot with hot water in the amount specified by the manufacturer (2 to 3 quarts is typical). Warm your jars by filling them with hot tap water and placing them near your cooking area. Prepare your rings and new lids by placing them in pairs (one new lid nested with one clean ring) nearby. Assemble the funnel and ladle, as well, and place a kitchen towel on the countertop next to the pressure canner.

4. Turn on the burner, the one on which the canner is sitting, to warm. Pour out the hot water from one jar. Ladle the hot mixture into the jar, leaving 1 inch of headspace. Add a sprig of rosemary or a few drops of rosemary oil to each jar.

(Continued on next page)

Apply new lids and rings fingertip tight to the jar and place it on the rack at the bottom of the pressure canner. Repeat the same procedure for each jar. Then, place the pressure canner lid on and secure according to the manufacturer's directions. Increase the heat to medium, and exhaust per the manufacturer's directions (typically for 10 minutes). Process at 11 pounds of pressure for 75 minutes for pint jars. When the time is up, turn the burner off and do *nothing* until the pressure valve on your pressure canner lid is completely released/flush with the lid and the dial indicates 0 pounds of pressure.

SPICY PEACH BARBEQUE CHICKEN

YIELD: 8 PINTS

These chicken chunks are right at home served on a freshly cooked bed of rice, offered up cold in a salad, or used as the main feature in a filling sandwich. Swap out jalapeños for bell peppers or other mild peppers if you'd prefer. This is one of the recipes that could easily be broken into days, or steps, where you roast the peppers one day and preserve the recipe the next.

YOU WILL NEED

3 bell peppers, ribs, seeds, and stems removed

Optional: 3 jalapeño peppers, ribs, seeds, and stems removed

3 large tomatoes, washed, cored, and chopped, juices reserved

¼ cup water

2 tablespoons olive oil

8 boneless, skinless chicken breasts, chopped

1 cup peach jam or preserves or fresh peaches, peeled and chopped

2 teaspoons salt

½ teaspoon pepper

2 teaspoons ground ginger

1 teaspoon ground allspice

1 tablespoon dry mustard

1 tablespoon fresh garlic, minced

½ cup brown sugar (packed)

¼ cup apple cider vinegar

¼ cup molasses

1. If you plan to use hot peppers, use gloves to protect your skin and do not touch your face. Wash your hands after handling hot peppers. My recommendation is for peppers to be left whole, as I find it easiest to turn whole peppers under heat (which you'll be doing next), but they can be halved.

2. First, blister the skins. This can be done in a variety of ways, but you essentially need to use heat to blister the skin of the peppers. Using the oven to blister the skins, place the peppers directly on the rack of an oven set to 400°F. Turn over with tongs carefully after 4 or 5 minutes for a total of 8 to 10 minutes in the oven. This method is my preferred option. Using the stovetop (either gas or electric) to blister the skins, use metal tongs to place peppers one at a time over the direct heat of the burner, blistering each pepper, rotating slowly over high heat. Remove each blistered pepper from the heat, place in a bowl, and cover with a lid or cloth. Let the peppers cool and sweat.

3. Once blistered and cooled, prepare to peel by washing the peppers. The skins can be peeled by hand or with the help of a knife. Remove the cores and seeds. (This is no doubt a time-consuming process best helped by a friend with whom you need to catch up, with a cold drink tableside!) Note: The blistering and peeling process can be done the day before you begin pressure canning.

4. Chop up the peppers and place them in a saucepan with the tomatoes and simmer with ¼ cup water over low heat for 30 minutes. Remove from heat and let cool.

(Continued on next page)

5. Puree the pepper and tomatoes by passing them through a food mill (this is my favorite method, as it removes skins and seeds) or by using a blender or immersion blender. Set aside.

6. Heat the oil in a large, heavy skillet over medium heat. Season the chicken with salt and pepper and brown the chicken on all sides. Transfer to a plate when the chicken is cooked halfway through or browned but still pink on the inside.

7. Return the pepper and tomato mixture to the saucepan and add the peach jam or preserves or fresh peaches, salt, pepper, ginger, allspice, sugar, vinegar, and molasses. Bring to a boil over medium-high heat, reduce to a simmer, and cook uncovered for about 30 minutes. Add the chicken back in and combine.

8. Prepare your pressure canner. Fill the pot with hot water in the amount specified by the manufacturer (2 to 3 quarts is typical). Warm your jars by filling them with hot tap water and placing them near your cooking area. Prepare your rings and new lids by placing them in pairs (one new lid nested with one clean ring) nearby. Assemble the funnel and ladle, as well, and place a kitchen towel on the countertop next to the pressure canner.

9. Turn on the burner, the one on which the canner is sitting, to warm. Pour out the hot water from one jar. Ladle the hot mixture into the jar, leaving 1 inch of headspace. Apply new lids and rings fingertip tight to the jar and place it on the rack at the bottom of the pressure canner. Repeat the same procedure for each jar. Then, place the pressure canner lid on and secure according to the manufacturer's directions. Increase the heat to medium, and exhaust per the manufacturer's directions (typically for 10 minutes). Process at 11 pounds of pressure for 75 minutes for pint jars. When the time is up, turn the burner off and do *nothing* until the pressure valve on your pressure canner lid is completely released/flush with the lid and the dial indicates 0 pounds of pressure.

KID-FRIENDLY SLOPPY JOES

YIELD: 4 PINTS

Feel free to season this joy-producing meal to suit the tastes of more adventurous eaters, if you'd like, but this rendition is mild enough to please the discerning palate of most any elementary school student.

YOU WILL NEED

1 tablespoon olive oil

½ onion, chopped

2 cloves garlic, minced

1 pound ground beef

2 cups dry black beans, soaked overnight and drained

1 teaspoon salt

¼–½ teaspoon chili powder

1 cup fresh tomatoes, chopped, or tomato sauce

1 tablespoon Worcestershire sauce

1 tablespoon brown sugar

1. Add the oil to a saucepan and heat to medium high, then add the onion and garlic and cook until translucent and browned a bit. Add the beef and brown. Add all remaining ingredients and cook till simmering.

2. Prepare your pressure canner. Fill the pot with hot water in the amount specified by the manufacturer (2 to 3 quarts is typical). Warm your jars by filling them with hot tap water and placing them near your cooking area. Prepare your rings and new lids by placing them in pairs (one new lid nested with one clean ring) nearby. Assemble the funnel and ladle, as well, and place a kitchen towel on the countertop next to the pressure canner.

3. Turn on the burner, the one on which the canner is sitting, to warm. Pour out the hot water from one jar. Ladle the hot mixture into the jar, leaving 1 inch of headspace. Apply new lids and rings fingertip tight to the jar and place it on the rack at the bottom of the pressure canner. Repeat the same procedure for each jar. Then, place the pressure canner lid on and secure according to the manufacturer's directions. Increase the heat to medium, and exhaust per the manufacturer's directions (typically for 10 minutes). Process at 11 pounds of pressure for 75 minutes for pint jars. When the time is up, turn the burner off and do *nothing* until the pressure valve on your pressure canner lid is completely released/flush with the lid and the dial indicates 0 pounds of pressure.

EVERY BEAN AND SAUSAGE SOUP

YIELD: 4 PINTS

The bean soup mixes found in most every grocery store offer a wide variety of bean colors, textures, sizes, and flavors, making this recipe more visually interesting and ideal to give to a friend. Pressure canning sausage as part of this soup makes it turn out extra *delicious, but it's important to drain the fat completely before canning, since extra fat will climb the sides of the jar and prohibit seal formation and will also interfere with even heat penetration.*

YOU WILL NEED

1 pound ground smoked low-fat sausage

2 cups dry mixed beans of choice, soaked 8 hours or overnight (Note: most bean mixes include pinto, kidney, lima, split pea, small white, yellow, and navy beans)

1 onion, diced

2 cups Basic Bone Broth (page 35), beef or chicken broth, or Vegetable Stock (page 41)

2 cups fresh tomatoes, diced, or 1 (14.5-ounce) can diced tomatoes

1 tablespoon garlic, chopped fine

1. Brown sausage over medium high heat in a stockpot and drain completely. Extra fat should be drained, as it interferes with a safe canning process. Combine all remaining ingredients and cook for 1 hour, until the beans and onion are tender. Note: These steps could be completed before canning, and canning could be done the following day, if desired.

2. Prepare your pressure canner. Fill the pot with hot water in the amount specified by the manufacturer (2 to 3 quarts is typical). Warm your jars by filling them with hot tap water and placing them near your cooking area. Prepare your rings and new lids by placing them in pairs (one new lid nested with one clean ring) nearby. Assemble the funnel and ladle, as well, and place a kitchen towel on the countertop next to the pressure canner.

3. Turn on the burner, the one on which the canner is sitting, to warm. Pour out the hot water from one jar. Ladle the hot soup into the jar, leaving 1 inch of headspace. Apply new lids and rings fingertip tight to the jar and place it on the rack at the bottom of the pressure canner. Repeat the same procedure for each jar. Then, place the pressure canner lid on and secure according to the manufacturer's directions. Increase the heat to medium, and exhaust per the manufacturer's directions (typically for 10 minutes). Process at 11 pounds of pressure for 75 minutes for pint jars. When the time is up, turn the burner off and do *nothing* until the pressure valve on your pressure canner lid is completely released/flush with the lid and the dial indicates 0 pounds of pressure.

EVERY BEAN AND HAM SOUP

YIELD: 4–5 PINTS

This is an excellent soup to make when there's leftover holiday ham in the house. A single cup of diced ham adds tons of flavor and makes for a filling and flavorful meal. Serve with a crusty slice of sourdough, or maybe a grilled cheese sandwich, ready to be dipped and thoroughly enjoyed!

YOU WILL NEED

2 cups dry mixed beans of choice, soaked 8 hours or overnight (Note: most bean mixes include pinto, kidney, lima, split pea, small white, yellow, and navy beans)

1 onion, diced

2 cups Basic Bone Broth (page 35), beef or chicken broth, or Vegetable Stock (page 41)

2 cups fresh tomatoes, diced, or 1 (14.5-ounce) can diced tomatoes

1 tablespoon garlic, chopped fine

1 cup cooked ham, chopped in ½-inch or smaller pieces

1 bay leaf

¼ teaspoon black peppercorns

1. Combine all ingredients and cook for 1 hour, until the beans and onion are tender.

2. Prepare your pressure canner. Fill the pot with hot water in the amount specified by the manufacturer (2 to 3 quarts is typical). Warm your jars by filling them with hot tap water and placing them near your cooking area. Prepare your rings and new lids by placing them in pairs (one new lid nested with one clean ring) nearby. Assemble the funnel and ladle, as well, and place a kitchen towel on the countertop next to the pressure canner.

3. Turn on the burner, the one on which the canner is sitting, to warm. Pour out the hot water from one jar. Ladle the hot soup into the jar, leaving 1 inch of headspace. Apply new lids and rings fingertip tight to the jar and place it on the rack at the bottom of the pressure canner. Repeat the same procedure for each jar. Then, place the pressure canner lid on and secure according to the manufacturer's directions. Increase the heat to medium, and exhaust per the manufacturer's directions (typically for 10 minutes). Process at 11 pounds of pressure for 75 minutes for pint jars. When the time is up, turn the burner off and do *nothing* until the pressure valve on your pressure canner lid is completely released/flush with the lid and the dial indicates 0 pounds of pressure.

MEXICAN BEAN AND BONE SOUP

YIELD: 5–6 PINTS

This soup recipe is truly one of my favorites in this book. Not only scrumptious—the bones and meat will release tons *of flavor—it's a frugal recipe, using inexpensive shank and bargain black beans. But together, with cumin and hominy, these jars shine alone, or as a perfect tortilla soup starter! Simply add a scoop of sour cream, guacamole, and a sprinkle of cheese upon reheating and you have an instant super supper (best served with tortilla chips, of course).*

YOU WILL NEED

2 cups black beans, soaked 8 hours or overnight and drained

2 meaty shank bones

1 cup celery, chopped, with optional celery greens mixed in

1 onion, chopped

2 cups fresh or canned tomatoes, chopped, juices reserved

1 cup hominy (soft, white corn-cousin kernels), drained

1 tablespoon garlic, chopped

2 tablespoons salt

1 teaspoon cumin

½ teaspoon chili powder

6 cups Basic Bone Broth (page 35), Vegetable Stock (page 41), or Plain Water (page 32), enough to cover all other ingredients with an inch of liquid

1. Combine all ingredients in a heavy pot or Dutch oven and cook 4+ hours on medium or low heat with the lid on, stirring occasionally. When the meat falls off the bones, remove from heat. Pull the bones from the pot, being sure to save every bit of meat.

2. Prepare your pressure canner. Fill the pot with hot water in the amount specified by the manufacturer (2 to 3 quarts is typical). Warm your jars by filling them with hot tap water and placing them near your cooking area. Prepare your rings and new lids by placing them in pairs (one new lid nested with one clean ring) nearby. Assemble the funnel and ladle, as well, and place a kitchen towel on the countertop next to the pressure canner.

3. Turn on the burner, the one on which the canner is sitting, to warm. Pour out the hot water from one jar. Ladle the hot soup into the jar, leaving 1 inch of headspace. Apply new lids and rings fingertip tight to the jar and place it on the rack at the bottom of the pressure canner. Repeat the same procedure for each jar. Then, place the pressure canner lid on and secure according to the manufacturer's directions. Increase the heat to medium, and exhaust per the manufacturer's directions (typically for 10 minutes). Process at 11 pounds of pressure for 75 minutes for pint jars. When the time is up, turn the burner off and do *nothing* until the pressure valve on your pressure canner lid is completely released/flush with the lid and the dial indicates 0 pounds of pressure.

POTATO SOUP BASE

YIELD: 4 QUARTS

This potato soup base can be easily blended upon opening the jars. It's a superbly warming and filling soup when a cold night calls for it!

YOU WILL NEED

6 russet potatoes, scrubbed, peeled, and chopped

1 onion, chopped

8 cups Basic Bone Broth (page 35), Vegetable Stock (page 41), or Plain Water (page 32)

3 stalks celery, chopped

3 carrots, peeled and chopped

1 tablespoon parsley, chopped

Optional: 1–3 drops liquid smoke

½ cup milk per quart

Dollop sour cream and crisp bacon, to garnish

1. Combine the potatoes, onion, broth or water, celery, carrots, parsley, and liquid smoke, if desired, in a stockpot and bring to a boil.

2. Prepare your pressure canner. Fill the pot with hot water in the amount specified by the manufacturer (2 to 3 quarts is typical). Warm your jars by filling them with hot tap water and placing them near your cooking area. Prepare your rings and new lids by placing them in pairs (one new lid nested with one clean ring) nearby. Assemble the funnel and ladle, as well, and place a kitchen towel on the countertop next to the pressure canner.

3. Turn on the burner, the one on which the canner is sitting, to warm. Pour out the hot water from one jar. Ladle the hot soup into the jar, leaving 1 inch of headspace. Apply new lids and rings fingertip tight to the jar and place it on the rack at the bottom of the pressure canner. Repeat the same procedure for each jar. Then, place the pressure canner lid on and secure according to the manufacturer's directions. Increase the heat to medium, and exhaust per the manufacturer's directions (typically for 10 minutes). Process at 11 pounds of pressure for 75 minutes for quart jars. When the time is up, turn the burner off and do *nothing* until the pressure valve on your pressure canner lid is completely released/flush with the lid and the dial indicates 0 pounds of pressure.

4. Upon reheating, add ½ cup milk per quart of soup and blend with an immersion blender. Add a dollop of sour cream, if desired, and top with crisp bacon.

ROASTED ROOT VEGGIES

YIELD: 4 PINTS

This tantalizing mix makes a great side dish. Note: Be sure to fill the jars and give them a side-to-side shimmy (using a potholder to protect your hand, of course) to encourage the pieces to settle down, as the jar's contents shrink significantly during the canning process.

YOU WILL NEED

4 yellow potatoes, peeled and diced in ½-inch chunks

2 tablespoons oil or more if needed

1 tablespoon salt, kosher preferred

1 large or 2 medium beet(s), peeled and diced in ½-inch chunks

3 large serrano peppers, ribs, seeds, and stems removed, chopped

3 banana or mild yellow peppers, ribs, seeds, and stems removed, chopped

1 onion, diced in ½-inch or smaller chunks

Optional: 1 sprig rosemary or 1–2 drops rosemary oil per pint jar

1. In a hot pan, brown the outside of the potatoes in the oil. Season potatoes with the kosher salt, and use a slotted spatula to transfer the potatoes to a plate when browned. Repeat with the beets. (You're precooking the root veggies to help them keep their shape and to give them great flavor.) Add a few more teaspoons of oil to the pan if needed to quickly brown the peppers and onions, then return all ingredients to the pan to incorporate.

2. Prepare your pressure canner. Fill the pot with hot water in the amount specified by the manufacturer (2 to 3 quarts is typical). Warm your jars by filling them with hot tap water and placing them near your cooking area. Prepare your rings and new lids by placing them in pairs (one new lid nested with one clean ring) nearby. Assemble the funnel and ladle, as well, and place a kitchen towel on the countertop next to the pressure canner.

3. Turn on the burner, the one on which the canner is sitting, to warm. Pour out the hot water from one jar. Ladle the hot vegetables into the jar and cover with hot water, leaving 1 inch of headspace. Add a sprig of rosemary or a few drops of rosemary oil to each jar. Apply new lids and rings fingertip tight to the jar and place it on the rack at the bottom of the pressure canner. Repeat the same procedure for each jar. Then, place the pressure canner lid on and secure according to the manufacturer's directions. Increase the heat to medium, and exhaust per the manufacturer's directions (typically for 10 minutes). Process at 11 pounds of pressure for 75 minutes for pint jars. When the time is up, turn the burner off and do *nothing* until the pressure valve on your pressure canner lid is completely released/flush with the lid and the dial indicates 0 pounds of pressure.

SPICY LAMB CHOPS

YIELD: 8 PINTS

Somewhat surprisingly, meat can be pressure canned with the bone in. However, I feel the bone takes up valuable space, so I typically take the time to remove it, making room for more meat. Since this recipe calls for roasted peppers, ground chili, and paprika, the result ends up being a powerhouse of flavor. Don't let the long ingredient list deter you, though; most of the ingredients are blended up into a spicy smoothie to be poured over the browned chunks of meat before they're canned. It's actually an easy recipe!

YOU WILL NEED

3 roasted red or green bell peppers (see directions on page 58)

1 tablespoon cumin

1 tablespoon ground coriander

1 teaspoon salt

¼ cup dried ground chili (I prefer to use dried ancho chili; I suggest you choose whatever smells amazing to you!)

¼ cup hot paprika or regular paprika, if you don't want this dish to be too spicy

2 teaspoons dried oregano

2 tablespoons garlic, minced

3 tablespoons red wine vinegar

2 tablespoons olive oil

16 (1-inch thick) lamb chops (with the bone cut out, if desired), cut so that all chunks of meat are about 1-inch thick in every direction

1. Puree the roasted peppers with the cumin, coriander, salt, chili, paprika, oregano, garlic, and red wine vinegar. Heat the olive oil in a skillet set to high. Season the lamb with salt and pepper and brown on all sides. Pour the roasted pepper mixture over the lamb chop chunks and stir to coat.

2. Prepare your pressure canner. Fill the pot with hot water in the amount specified by the manufacturer (2 to 3 quarts is typical). Warm your jars by filling them with hot tap water and placing them near your cooking area. Prepare your rings and new lids by placing them in pairs (one new lid nested with one clean ring) nearby. Assemble the funnel and ladle, as well, and place a kitchen towel on the countertop next to the pressure canner.

3. Turn on the burner, the one on which the canner is sitting, to warm. Pour out the hot water from one jar. Ladle the mixture into jar, leaving 1 inch of headspace. Apply new lids and rings fingertip tight to the jar and place it on the rack at the bottom of the pressure canner. Repeat the same procedure for each jar. Then, place the pressure canner lid on and secure according to the manufacturer's directions. Increase the heat to medium, and exhaust per the manufacturer's directions (typically for 10 minutes). Process at 11 pounds of pressure for 75 minutes for pint jars. When the time is up, turn the burner off and do *nothing* until the pressure valve on your pressure canner lid is completely released/flush with the lid and the dial indicates 0 pounds of pressure.

Rivers, Lakes, and the Sea: Fish in Jars

Fish can be preserved in a pressure canner, just as red meat can, but it calls for the longest processing times of any recipe you'll find: one hundred minutes for pint jars. The time commitment is worth it, though, as the fresh taste of wild-caught fish *and* the quality therein cannot be beat! Even a humble tuna sandwich becomes extra delicious when made with home-canned, fresh-caught fish.

HALIBUT, MACKEREL, SALMON, STEELHEAD TROUT, AND OTHER FATTY FISH

YIELD: 1 POUND FISH = ABOUT 1 PINT

Before proceeding, there are some special details to note about canning fish. The fact is, I've read tested, safe directions for canning quarts of fish, yet I've never done it. Why not? The processing time is astronomical (more than two and a half hours), plus additional steps are required for filling the pressure canner with more than a typical amount of water. After reflecting on the matter, I eventually decided canned pints are sufficient and best for this book, especially in the name of simplicity, so I've chosen not to include any of those tested, safe canning-in-quarts directions in this book. If pressure canning quarts of fish is important to you, I suggest following the directions from your local university cooperative extension office on canning quarts of fish.

Please also note that salmon, when canned, can develop glassy crystals of struvite, which is magnesium phosphate. These crystals are safe, and there's no way to prevent them from forming. Interestingly, I've never had them form when I can, but it's important to know it could happen to you . . . and not to worry if it does. FYI: The crystals usually dissolve when heated. You'll just need to check the rim of the jar extra carefully for fish oil before adding the new lids, since oil is another one of the enemies of a good seal. Use a funnel (as you would with every recipe in this book, and every canning recipe) and wipe each rim carefully.

Remember that all fish should be kept cold until ready to can.

YOU WILL NEED

Fresh fish, rinsed with water
(Helpful hint: Add ½ cup white vinegar to 1 gallon of rinsing water if the fish is slimy; the vinegar will help remove the slime)

Optional: 1 teaspoon salt per pint jar

1. You can preserve fish with the skin on, if you like (unless you're canning halibut, in which case, it's best to remove the skin), *and* you don't have to remove bones, as the processing will cause them to become very soft/dissolved and they'll simply add more calcium to the fish when consumed.

2. Remove the head, tail, fins, and all innards. Cut fish into pieces that are no longer than 3 inches in length.

3. Prepare your pressure canner. Fill the pot with hot water in the amount specified by the manufacturer (2 to 3 quarts is typical). Warm your jars by filling them with hot tap water and placing them near your cooking area. Prepare your rings and new lids by placing them in pairs (one new lid nested with one clean ring) nearby. Assemble the funnel and ladle, as well, and place a kitchen towel on the countertop next to the pressure canner.

4. Turn on the burner, the one on which the canner is sitting, to warm. Pour out the hot water from one jar. Ladle pieces of fish into jar, leaving 1 inch of headspace. Add 1 teaspoon salt per pint, if desired. Do not add water or other liquids. Apply new lids and rings fingertip tight to the jar and place it on the rack at the bottom of the pressure canner. Repeat the same procedure for each jar. Then, place the pressure canner lid on and secure according to the manufacturer's directions. Increase the heat to medium, and exhaust per the manufacturer's directions (typically for 10 minutes). Process at 11 pounds of pressure for 100 minutes for pint jars. Fish canned in half pints (resembling closely in size store-bought cans of fish) should also be processed for 100 minutes. When the time is up, turn the burner off and do *nothing* until the pressure valve on your pressure canner lid is completely released/flush with the lid and the dial indicates 0 pounds of pressure.

TUNA

YIELD: 1 POUND FISH = ABOUT 1 PINT

A few preliminary notes: First, it's preferable to pressure can the lighter flesh of the tuna, while the darker flesh is best not canned. Second, it's safe to raw pack tuna, but the result of hot pack tuna is much better tasting and preferred by many. Third, the cooked tuna meat needs to be refrigerated overnight after cooking, before it's pressure canned, making it a somewhat unique cold hot-pack process. You'll be shocked, perhaps, to learn you can cover your tuna in oil and can it safely in a pressure canner. I like to can my tuna in water, but if you choose to can in oil, make sure you wipe off every smidge of oil from the rim of the jar, as oil can prevent a seal from forming. Tuna can be canned in half pint jars to be enjoyed or gifted in sizes similar to that of a store-bought can of tuna!

YOU WILL NEED

Fresh tuna, rinsed with
　water
Optional: 1 teaspoon salt
　per pint jar
Optional: olive oil, to cover
　contents of each jar

1. Preheat oven to 350°F. Grease a baking dish to prevent the tuna from sticking, add your tuna to the baking dish, and bake for 1 hour, until a 165°F internal temperature is reached. Refrigerate meat overnight.

2. The next day, peel the tuna skin off, remove any blood vessels and dark sections of meat, and cut meat away from the bones. Pull out all the bones you can. Cut your deboned, light meat into chunks that are about 2 inches long.

3. Prepare your pressure canner. Fill the pot with hot water in the amount specified by the manufacturer (2 to 3 quarts is typical). Warm your jars by filling them with hot tap water and placing them near your cooking area. Prepare your rings and new lids by placing them in pairs (one new lid nested with one clean ring) nearby. Assemble the funnel and ladle, as well, and place a kitchen towel on the countertop next to the pressure canner.

4. Turn on the burner, the one on which the canner is sitting, to warm. Pour out the hot water from one jar. Ladle cooked tuna pieces into the jar, leaving 1 inch of headspace. Add 1 teaspoon salt per pint, if desired. Cover cooked tuna pieces with water or olive oil, maintaining 1 inch of headspace. Apply new lids and rings fingertip tight to the jar and place it on the rack at the bottom of the pressure canner. Repeat the same procedure for each jar. Then, place the pressure canner lid on and secure according to the manufacturer's directions. Increase the heat to medium, and exhaust per the

manufacturer's directions (typically for 10 minutes). Process at 11 pounds of pressure for 100 minutes for both half pints and pint jars. When the time is up, turn the burner off and do *nothing* until the pressure valve on your pressure canner lid is completely released/flush with the lid and the dial indicates 0 pounds of pressure.

GARLIC AND HERB TILAPIA

YIELD: 4 HALF PINTS

Tilapia is mild in flavor, readily available in stores, and a good source of protein. I love to can half pint jars of this fish, seasoned with a classic mix of garlic and herbs to be added to salads and sandwiches.

YOU WILL NEED

1 pound tilapia, fresh or freshly defrosted, no skin

1 tablespoon dried Italian seasoning

1 tablespoon minced garlic

½ teaspoon salt

1. Cut tilapia into pieces that are 1 to 2 inches long, and no thicker than an inch. Sprinkle the remaining ingredients evenly over the fish.

2. Prepare your pressure canner. Fill the pot with hot water in the amount specified by the manufacturer (2 to 3 quarts is typical). Warm your jars by filling them with hot tap water and placing them near your cooking area. Prepare your rings and new lids by placing them in pairs (one new lid nested with one clean ring) nearby. Assemble the funnel and ladle, as well, and place a kitchen towel on the countertop next to the pressure canner.

3. Turn on the burner, the one on which the canner is sitting, to warm. Pour out the hot water from one jar. Ladle the tilapia into the jar, leaving 1 inch of headspace. Do not add water or other liquids. Apply new lids and rings fingertip tight to the jar and place it on the rack at the bottom of the pressure canner. Repeat the same procedure for each jar. Then, place the pressure canner lid on and secure according to the manufacturer's directions. Increase the heat to medium, and exhaust per the manufacturer's directions (typically for 10 minutes). Process at 11 pounds of pressure for 100 minutes for half pints or pint jars. When the time is up, turn the burner off and do *nothing* until the pressure valve on your pressure canner lid is completely released/flush with the lid and the dial indicates 0 pounds of pressure.

FISH TACO TILAPIA

YIELD: 4 HALF PINTS

Tilapia makes an effective vehicle for flavor in these spicy jars. Reduce the cayenne for less heat, if you wish, and enjoy in tacos, salads, and more!

YOU WILL NEED

1 pound tilapia, fresh or freshly defrosted, no skin

1 teaspoon red pepper flakes

2 teaspoons cumin

1 teaspoon paprika

1 teaspoon chili powder

1. Cut tilapia into pieces that are 1 to 2 inches long, and no thicker than an inch. Sprinkle the remaining ingredients evenly over the fish.

2. Prepare your pressure canner. Fill the pot with hot water in the amount specified by the manufacturer (2 to 3 quarts is typical). Warm your jars by filling them with hot tap water and placing them near your cooking area. Prepare your rings and new lids by placing them in pairs (one new lid nested with one clean ring) nearby. Assemble the funnel and ladle, as well, and place a kitchen towel on the countertop next to the pressure canner.

3. Turn on the burner, the one on which the canner is sitting, to warm. Pour out the hot water from one jar. Ladle the tilapia into the jar, leaving 1 inch of headspace. Do not add water or other liquids. Apply new lids and rings fingertip tight to the jar and place it on the rack at the bottom of the pressure canner. Repeat the same procedure for each jar. Then, place the pressure canner lid on and secure according to the manufacturer's directions. Increase the heat to medium, and exhaust per the manufacturer's directions (typically for 10 minutes). Process at 11 pounds of pressure for 100 minutes for half pints or pint jars. When the time is up, turn the burner off and do *nothing* until the pressure valve on your pressure canner lid is completely released/flush with the lid and the dial indicates 0 pounds of pressure.

YELLOWFIN TUNA

YIELD: 4 HALF PINTS

This is the most versatile of the fish recipes, I think, because it's primed to be turned into a classic tuna sandwich, and it's also perfect for enhancing salads and other dishes, as well! (Try it on an everything bagel for a filling lunch.)

YOU WILL NEED

1 pound yellowfin tuna, skin and bones removed

4 tablespoons lemon juice

1 teaspoon peppercorns

½ teaspoon salt

1. Cut the tuna into pieces that are 1 to 2 inches long, and no thicker than an inch. Sprinkle the remaining ingredients evenly over the fish.

2. Prepare your pressure canner. Fill the pot with hot water in the amount specified by the manufacturer (2 to 3 quarts is typical). Warm your jars by filling them with hot tap water and placing them near your cooking area. Prepare your rings and new lids by placing them in pairs (one new lid nested with one clean ring) nearby. Assemble the funnel and ladle, as well, and place a kitchen towel on the countertop next to the pressure canner.

3. Turn on the burner, the one on which the canner is sitting, to warm. Pour out the hot water from one jar. Ladle the tuna into the jar, leaving 1 inch of headspace. Do not add water or other liquids. Apply new lids and rings fingertip tight to the jar and place it on the rack at the bottom of the pressure canner. Repeat the same procedure for each jar. Then, place the pressure canner lid on and secure according to the manufacturer's directions. Increase the heat to medium, and exhaust per the manufacturer's directions (typically for 10 minutes). Process at 11 pounds of pressure for 100 minutes for half pints or pint jars. When the time is up, turn the burner off and do *nothing* until the pressure valve on your pressure canner lid is completely released/flush with the lid and the dial indicates 0 pounds of pressure.

GRAVLAX-STYLE SALMON

YIELD: 4 HALF PINTS

While this isn't a true gravlax, absent the tequila, this particular flavor combination truly sings in these jars! It's a fresh, bright, and delicious way to preserve a Pacific Northwest classic.

YOU WILL NEED

1 pound salmon, skin and bones removed

4 tablespoons lime juice

2 tablespoons salt

1 tablespoons sugar

1. Cut the salmon into pieces that are 1 to 2 inches long, and no thicker than an inch. Sprinkle the remaining ingredients evenly over the fish.

2. Prepare your pressure canner. Fill the pot with hot water in the amount specified by the manufacturer (2 to 3 quarts is typical). Warm your jars by filling them with hot tap water and placing them near your cooking area. Prepare your rings and new lids by placing them in pairs (one new lid nested with one clean ring) nearby. Assemble the funnel and ladle, as well, and place a kitchen towel on the countertop next to the pressure canner.

3. Turn on the burner, the one on which the canner is sitting, to warm. Pour out the hot water from one jar. Ladle the salmon into jar, leaving 1 inch of headspace. Do not add water or other liquids. Apply new lids and rings fingertip tight to the jar and place it on the rack at the bottom of the pressure canner. Repeat the same procedure for each jar. Then, place the pressure canner lid on and secure according to the manufacturer's directions. Increase the heat to medium, and exhaust per the manufacturer's directions (typically for 10 minutes). Process at 11 pounds of pressure for 100 minutes for half pints or pint jars. When the time is up, turn the burner off and do *nothing* until the pressure valve on your pressure canner lid is completely released/flush with the lid and the dial indicates 0 pounds of pressure.

CONCLUDING NOTES AND MESSAGE FROM JENNY, MASTER FOOD PRESERVER

While you've now arrived here at the end of this book, it's surely not the end of your pressure canning journey. I encourage you to venture forth, learning as you go, seeking tested, safe recipes, inviting preserving friends or family members to join in, and adventuring onward in your pressure canning practice. And it *is* exactly that: a practice.

From time to time, I have jars that fail to seal, or a jar that breaks in the canner, or a mystery "challenge" I can't quite figure out. This is normal, no matter how frustrating it can be. Keep studying and observing, keep working at the process, and while practice won't necessarily "make perfect," it *will* make for great progress.

If you've read this book all the way through and now aren't sure what to can, or in what order, here are a few ideas to get you started.

If you've never canned before:
Can Plain Water (page 32), then try Vegetable Stock (page 41), followed by Ground Beef (page 81).

If you've canned a few times prior, but are still new to pressure canning:
Can Roasted Mushroom Stock (page 42), then French Onion Soup (page 47), followed by Crushed Tomatoes (page 63).

If you're an intermediate canner:
Can Basic Bone Broth (page 35) and consider hosting a bone broth party with friends! If you're inclined to give it a go, try the Perfectly Preserved Bloody Mary (page 67) with all the fixings, then try Mexican Bean and Bone Soup (page 116), followed by Gravlax-Style Salmon (page 133).

If you're eager to can recipes beyond this book, search for pressure canning recipes from any cooperative extension office or website, as you'll know they're tested and safe.

This is me signing off, but I'll be standing by your side in spirit—as you chop veggies, peel tomatoes, and fill jars—encouraging you every step of the way!

SPECIAL THANKS

A good editor is critical to the writing process, but a great editor will also fan the flame inside a writer until it's a roaring fire, and that is what my editor and writing coach Willy Mathes has done for me. Thank you for helping me see I am, and how to be, a writer.

I met Anna Cash of Smart Home Canning online, as we were both sharing our canning enthusiasm with our respective social media audiences and on our blogs. Not only did Anna befriend me, but she also invited me to her home so I could take the Master Preserver Course in Utah. We then joined forces to create and cohost the *Perfectly Preserved Podcast*. I couldn't ask for a better canning friend or podcast cohost, and there's no one who cans better pepper jelly than Anna Cash!

Thanks so much to all my friends, near and far, for supporting me.

And thank you, once again, to my family for . . . everything! There's only room for one at the computer keyboard, but it's a lot less lonely knowing I have the support and love of my husband and children, who are especially deserving of my heartfelt appreciation. I love you.

METRIC CONVERSIONS

If you're accustomed to using metric measurements, use these handy charts to convert the imperial measurements used in this book.

Weight (Dry Ingredients)

1 oz		30 g
4 oz	¼ lb	120 g
8 oz	½ lb	240 g
12 oz	¾ lb	360 g
16 oz	1 lb	480 g
32 oz	2 lb	960 g

Oven Temperatures

Fahrenheit	Celsius	Gas Mark
225°	110°	¼
250°	120°	½
275°	140°	1
300°	150°	2
325°	160°	3
350°	180°	4
375°	190°	5
400°	200°	6
425°	220°	7
450°	230°	8

Volume (Liquid Ingredients)

½ tsp.		2 ml
1 tsp.		5 ml
1 Tbsp.	½ fl oz	15 ml
2 Tbsp.	1 fl oz	30 ml
¼ cup	2 fl oz	60 ml
⅓ cup	3 fl oz	80 ml
½ cup	4 fl oz	120 ml
⅔ cup	5 fl oz	160 ml
¾ cup	6 fl oz	180 ml
1 cup	8 fl oz	240 ml
1 pt	16 fl oz	480 ml
1 qt	32 fl oz	960 ml

Length

¼ in	6 mm
½ in	13 mm
¾ in	19 mm
1 in	25 mm
6 in	15 cm
12 in	30 cm

INDEX